4

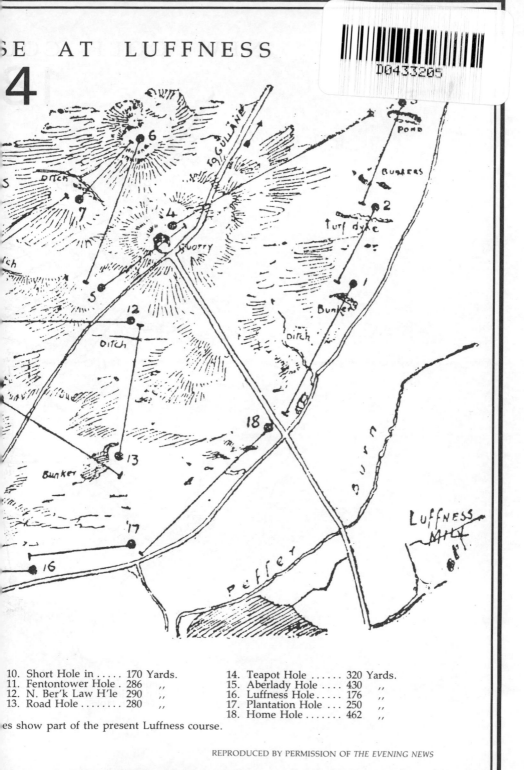

10. Short Hole in . . . . . 170 Yards.
11. Fentontower Hole . 286 ,,
12. N. Ber'k Law H'le 290 ,,
13. Road Hole . . . . 280 ,,

14. Teapot Hole . . . . . . 320 Yards.
15. Aberlady Hole . . . . 430 ,,
16. Luffness Hole . . . . . 176 ,,
17. Plantation Hole . . . 250 ,,
18. Home Hole . . . . 462 ,,

es show part of the present Luffness course.

ONE HUNDRED YEARS AT LUFFNESS NEW
1894-1994

Luffness New Golf Clubhouse, circa 1920.

Editor
W. Donald MacLennan

First Published 1994
by Luffness New Golf Club

This copy is number

784

Macdonald Lindsay Pindar plc
Edgefield Road, Loanhead,
Midlothian EH20 9SY

CONTENTS

iii

LIST OF ILLUSTRATIONS

FOREWORD

There are certain things which you never forget. My early acquaintance with Luffness is one of them.

In the impressionable years of boyhood, there was nothing like a round on an unfamiliar course to prove there is life beyond your own Club. Luffness sparked off the exploring instinct that is half the fun of golf, but there are many other happy memories.

Appreciation of the kindness of those who introduced my brother and me to the delights of an incomparable links. A lunch that, compared to the institutional fare to which we were used at school, was a veritable feast; and a friendly atmosphere in the Club that you could spot a mile off.

In spite of making the journey through Aberlady countless times since, that sense of expectation lingers, for Luffness typifies the best of British golf. The course occupies the most natural piece of golfing land in the world and the members a body determined to enjoy it to the full.

At a time when so many golf course architects believe in moving heaven and earth during construction, Luffness is a monument to the opposing school which happily accepts what it finds. Although Luffness houses the qualifying rounds for the Open Championship, its main purpose is to serve the needs of its members and visitors. Not for them island greens surrounded by water, lakes on every other hole, and a succession of problems far beyond the average player.

Luffness can be hard—mighty hard—when the wind whistles down the Forth and the rough is thick enough to whet the whistle of a hungry herd. There are distinctive bunkers, too, but, like all great courses, Luffness rewards the virtues. It is honest and straightforward and, to an inexperienced golfer in his teens, as I was in the early 1950s, possessed the best greens imaginable. Subsequent visits have shown them to be every bit as good as I think I remember them but, apart from the disappearance of the short 6th, happily nothing has changed.

On good days and bad, Luffness offers a feeling of escape allied to a sense of challenge and enjoyment that few other courses can match.

Donald Steel

International Golf Course Architect.

INTRODUCTION

As the reader of this book will discover if he does not already know, golf has been played in the area around Luffness since the sixteenth century. In these terms Luffness New Golf Club is a youngster, but in its relatively short life it has a proud story to tell and as the Club celebrates its centenary this book formally marks the occasion.

There may be some members for whom golf is what Luffness is all about but for me, and I suspect the great majority of members, it is a composite of many things that makes Luffness New Golf Club what it is.

— The friendliness of the members and staff; and the characters that help to give the Club its personality.

— The history and traditions which set the standards and style with which we play and conduct ourselves.

— The surroundings, the panoramic views of Arthur's Seat to the west, Gullane and the Fife hills to the north and the setting sun of a winter's evening over Aberlady Bay.

— The wildlife, never forgetting the arrival of the geese in September.

— Inevitably, the course and its renowned greens, meticulously tended by the head greenkeeper and his staff.

— And much more. . . .

This book cleverly weaves together all the strands that go to tell the story of Luffness.

To Professor W. Donald MacLennan (Bill to his fellow members) and all those who have contributed directly through the content of this book or their "off-stage" support, we are greatly indebted.

As Bill's dinner match opponents will readily testify, he meets challenges head on and in editing this book through the last one and a half years he has shown the same tenacity of purpose and has committed an enormous amount of time to ensuring its successful and timely completion. So to Bill I would like to give a special acknowledgement for his skill and application, as perhaps one might expect of a successful oral surgeon, in putting together "One Hundred Years at Luffness New"—a story to be proud of.

Nigel B. Richardson,
Captain, Luffness New Golf Club.

LUFFNESS FROM ABERLADY

THE STORY OF LUFFNESS

by

NIGEL TRANTER

This whole area of Luffness, Aberlady Bay and Gullane, has a resounding history, and from earliest times. Incidentally, the name is usually mispronounced, or at least mis-accented. Most folk call it Luff**ness**, the accent on the ness; whereas it ought to be **Luff**ness. Probably this mistake is caused by the pronunciation of more widely-known places, such as Inverness, where the accent **is** on the last syllable. Ness, of course, here is just a form of the Norse word for nose, or point. In Inverness it is the name of the loch and river, inver like aber meaning at the mouth of. And Luff is a corruption of Lofda. The story, dating from the 9th century, refers to a typical Viking raid by the notorious Anlaf the Dane. One of the henchmen was called Lofda, and he was slain here, and actually buried beneath the floor of what is now Luffness House. So that is how your Club got its name—Lofda's Nose or Point.

That point or minor headland no longer exists, of course, for Aberlady Bay is one of the strangest and most interesting major features of the east coast of Scotland, in that it is continually changing its shape, and indeed contracting. Once it was fully twice the size that it is today, and with its salt waters reaching far inland eastwards—where your clubhouse is indeed. That is how Saltcoats got its name, for there were placed the salt-pans, where the sea-water was heated to evaporate and leave the salt, this done by the monks of Luffness Priory. So the tide came quite far up the Vale of Peffer. Today the bay is still shrinking, by many acres every year or so. This is caused by

1

the soft washed-up sand on the great sand-bar, over two miles long and half-a-mile wide, at the mouth of the bay, where the wild-geese roost. This area, dried out at low tide, the prevailing westerly winds blow the sand in drifts eastwards towards Gullane; and this sand catches on flotsam and jetsam, and nowadays on all but indestructible plastics, to form little mounds; marram-grass seeds itself on these mounds, and these catch more blown sand, and grow into dunes, high dunes, these ever encroaching and lessening the area of the bay. In another fifty years . . . ?

So Aberlady Bay is notable for more than its teeming birdlife and wild flora. Many botanists come here to examine the especial kinds of plant-life, all notably prickly, which grow in the first few years on the newly-created land and nowhere else, binding the sand and putting down a sort of turf-bed—prickly, so that they are not eaten by herbivores, Nature's way of prevailing land over water. Incidentally, the name Aberlady is nowadays nearly always mispronounced too, at least from its original. It has nothing to do with Our Lady, the Virgin Mary, as is often assumed. Aber refers to the mouth of the Peffer Burn. And ledaig means a flat place. So that river-mouth at a flat place is an eminently suitable descriptive name. And some of the long-time locals still call it Aberledy.

The bay, when it was twice as large as it is now, was more than twice as deep also, the Peffer Burn having brought down and deposited vast quantities of our East Lothian topsoil. So that once Aberlady was the port of Haddington, and sizeable shipping could tie up on the west or Kilspindie side. The squarish stone building in front of your predecessor Golf Club, Kilspindie, was actually the custom-house of the port. The name Kilspindie, believe it or not, comes from kil, meaning the cell, or chapel of a Celtic saint; and that saint was St Pensandus.

The earliest reference or record of the Luffness-Aberlady area goes further back than Lofda or even Pensandus, back to the early 6th century, when Thanea enhances our East Lothian story. She was the daughter of King Loth, who gave name to Lothian, a minor Celtic monarch. He would have had Thanea wed a princeling called Owen, whom the girl rejected, partly because she did not like him and partly because he was not a Christian, as she was—although King Loth's faith had lapsed. Anyway, her father was angry, and sent her to be what amounted to a slave for his chief shepherd in the Lammermuirs, as punishment. But Owen went and raped her there. Pregnant, King Loth was the more furious, and ordered her death—for this was the penalty of high-born young women illegitimately pregnant. He had her cast over the precipitous south face of Traprain Law—on which he had his fortress-capital. However, she survived; and, afraid that her Christian God was taking an interest, and might make things uncomfortable for himself, Loth decided to hand his daugther over to Manannan, the sea-god—where Clackmannan gets its name—and

2

had her taken down to Aberlady Bay, put in a coracle, without a paddle, and cast adrift to Manannan. She drifted out as far as the Isle of May, the tide turned, and the coracle was carried up-Forth, to ground at Culross, where St Serf had his monastery. That Celtic saint took in the poor girl, and there her son was born. He was given the name of Kentigern, although Serf affectionately called him Mungo, meaning mannikin. And in due course Mungo himself became a Celtic missionary, and moved west with his mother, to the Clyde, to found *his* establishment, which became Eglaid-cu, or Glasgow. His grave is still below St Mungo's Cathedral there.

So you see what our area is responsible for! Glasgow folk cannot spell, of course, and called Thanea St Enoch.

Luffness became important in a different way in the 12th century, when the Earls of Dunbar and March were given most of what is now East Lothian, and set up a very strong castle at the head of Aberlady Bay. Today, the old part of Luffness House looks like a fairly typical late 16th-century tower-house. But in fact its lower storeys are part of the main keep of a large fortress-type stronghold of three centuries earlier, the moat of which, with the foundations of four angle-towers, are still there.

Luffness passed by marriage to the Lindsay family in the 13th century, and came into prominence when Sir David de Lindsay, who sat in the Scots parliament as Baron of Luffness, became Regent for young King Alexander the Third, who succeeded to the throne at the age of seven. So Alexander was often at Luffness, and much of importance must have taken place there. When the King came of age and no longer required a Regent, Sir David went on Crusade to the Holy Land, like so many another. Falling sick at Acre, as did others, probably of malaria, he was nursed by one of the monks dispossessed by the Saracens from the Mount Carmel monastery. This was a fellow-Scot, one of the Lauders of the Bass—the ruins of their little castle can still be seen on the Bass Rock. Dying, Lindsay told Lauder that if he would have his body embalmed and shipped back to Luffness for proper burial, his brother would give him land there to set up a new monastery of his own. This was in 1264. It took four years to get the body back and the chapel of the monastery built— allegedly the first Carmelite establishment in Scotland—and Sir David's stone coffin and recumbent effigy are still to be seen in the ruined chapel just 200 yards behind my house.

The Lindsays grew in greatness after that, becoming Earls of Crawford and marrying into the royal family, with many estates. They appointed a line of hereditary keepers for Luffness, named Bickerton. These Bickertons also played their part in the nation's story, one a grim part indeed, stabbing the Earl of Douglas in the back at the Battle of Otterburn, the occasion when a "dead man won the battle".

But in 1549 Luffness achieved great fame again in a very different way, when an English army was besieged in Haddington and a fleet was sent up to Aberlady Bay to try to relieve it. This was kept at bay in more senses than one, however, by cannon fired from Luffness Castle, and had to retire unsuccessful. Later in revenge, the Lord Protector Somerset, after the Treaty of Haddington, managed to have Luffness Castle "spoiled". But the walling of the keep's lower storey was, and is, ten feet thick, and resisted total demolition, although the curtain-walls and angle-towers were cast down. So the place remained in ruins until, in 1584, Sir Patrick Hepburn of Waughton, gaining the monastic land nearby at the Reformation, rebuilt the castle as it now is. His initials S.P.H. and the date 1584, appear on one of the turrets still.

The Hope family came to Luffness in the early 18th century, and happily, are still there. It was one of them who was responsible for founding your Club.

The other castle nearby, of course, is Saltcoats, also founded just post-Reformation, on the monks' lands. It came to the Lethington family then, a branch from the property which is now called Lennoxlove. The story is told that the first of the line gained the lands partly as reward for killing a wild boar which was terrorising the good folk of Gullane. The hand-spear and gauntlet-glove with which he performed this feat used to be kept in Dirleton Kirk until its renovation in 1825, when it disappeared..

Why Dirleton, not Gullane? This is accounted for by the fact that, in James the Sixth's reign, the parish kirk was transferred from Gullane to Dirleton—not as is usually declared because the King disapproved of the minister smoking tobacco—but for the convenience of his friend Sir Thomas Erskine, who so aided him at the Gowrie Conspiracy of ill repute, and was made Earl of Kellie and Viscount Fentoun, and given Dirleton estate for his services. He preferred to have the kirk nearby!

Yet Gullane's ancient church of St Andrew is still there, sadly ruined and abandoned, and should be restored as a show-place. It was a famous establishment, dating from Knights Templar times—there are still Templar names perpetuated in Gullane. Later, when that Order was brought low, it became the Collegiate Church, with no fewer than eight subsidiary priests and a Provost. A field east of Gullane is still called College Park—to the perplexity of some of the villagers.

But—enough is enough. Luffness's story will no doubt go on, let us hope worthily of its resounding past. Is that too much to hope for?

1894-1994

A CHRONOLOGICAL HISTORY OF THE CLUB

by

JAMES FALCONER

Why Luffness—Why "New"?

1894

Robert Louis Stevenson died on the island of Samoa.
Gladstone resigned as Prime Minister.
The Manchester Ship Canal was opened.
Luffness New Golf Club was founded.

It is thought that golf has been played at Aberlady from about the 16th century and James V (1513-1542), father of Mary Queen of Scots, is said to have played golf on Gosford Estate to the west of Luffness Estate. For many years the first Monday of the year, known as Handsel Monday, was celebrated as a gala day throughout East Lothian and a game of golf was frequently part of the festivities. It is believed that a club called Kilspindie Club was in existence in the early part of the 19th century. Membership was entirely of local people who played golf on rough ground and bents on what became known as the Wanster Course. There do not appear to be any records of this Club and it is not known when it was started.

In the latter half of the 19th century the Volunteer Movement became very active and a rifle range was laid out on the Wanster Course for use by The Aberlady Company of Volunteers. This seems to have been partly responsible for the break-up of this Kilspindie Club as the range interfered with the use of the links as a golf course. Also many members were enticed away from the game by the attractions of rifle-shooting. The Club was eventually wound up and those who wanted to continue playing golf endeavoured to get a game at Gullane. It is reported that they were not very well received by the Gullane locals and being anxious to find a game nearer home, they started playing on the links near to Luffness House. This led to an approach being made in October 1867 to Mr Henry Walter Hope of Luffness, for a golf course to be made there.

On 24 October 1867 a meeting was held in the office of Mr Peter Brown, Aberlady, at which Mr Hope's formal permission was given for the playing of golf on Luffness Links. This was to be entirely at his pleasure and on payment of rent of one shilling per annum. At that meeting it was resolved that a club be formed, open to all residents of East Lothian, at an annual subscription of five shillings. It was further resolved that the club be called Luffness Golf Club.

In conjunction with Mr Hope a course was laid out by Mr Tom Morris, Senior, and the first competition was able to be held at the end of November 1867. A report on that event in the *Haddingtonshire Courier* states:

> "There was a considerable muster of players on the occasion, among whom was the celebrated player Thomas Morris of St Andrews, who acted as umpire in the game. About ten o'clock the first couple, Mr P. Brown and Mr Congalton started, and were followed in close succession by other competitors. It was found that when the course had been played over, the lowest score was Mr P. Hunter with 108 for seventeen holes."

It was only about 1872 when an extra hole was added to bring the number to 18.

In January 1868 the Rev. J. H. Tait of Aberlady was admitted as a member and later that year he presented a "Silver Miniature Play Club" as a trophy to be played for annually on 26 September which was the anniversary of his ordination as Minister of the Parish of Aberlady.

Social events played an important part in the Club calendar and the *Haddingtonshire Courier* of 25 September 1868 reported on the first social gathering of the Club, recently held at the Golf Inn, Aberlady. This was attended by the Club President, Mr Henry W. Hope of Luffness, the Rt Hon. Lord Elcho, M.P., the Rev. J. H. Tait together with about forty to fifty members and friends.

Many improvements were made to the course in the early years whilst a new stone clubhouse was built to replace the original small building. The clubhouse was just across the bridge spanning the Peffer Burn, near to the 1st tee and not far from the 18th green. Competitions and matches were soon inaugurated and the Minutes of May 1874 make the following reference to a match against Glasgow Golf Club:

> "Nine members played on each side, the Glasgow Club won the first round by 39 holes and the Luffness Club the second by 5 holes leaving a majority in favour of Glasgow of 34 holes."

Luffness G.C. Clubhouse situated across the Peffer Burn—Members ready for a game.

In 1883 the first signs of discord appeared when the Club President, Mr Henry W. Hope, returned home after a long absence abroad. He was concerned to find that the Club had grown much larger than he anticipated when he first granted the right in 1867 to the playing of golf on his Estate. Also, the number of non-local members was larger than expected. In brief, he wanted a power of veto over club affairs. As a large part of the course was on his land he was anxious to safeguard his property rights. Somewhat reluctantly the Club agreed to the conditions laid down by Mr Hope. Further difficulties arose in 1888 when the Agents for Luffness Estate informed the Club that the privilege of playing golf over Luffness golf links would be withdrawn after 24 October 1888. However, negotiations took place and the Club's lease was renewed until Martinmas 1898. It is perhaps pertinent to note here that although the members of Luffness Golf Club met the running costs of the Club, Mr Hope had borne the original cost of laying out the golf course and over the years had made several generous gifts to the Club.

It may be of interest that in May 1890 a query was raised by the Club regarding amateur status when the following definition was given by the Royal and Ancient Golf Club of St Andrews:

> "An amateur golfer shall be a golfer who has never made for sale golf clubs or any other article connected with the game, who has never carried clubs for hire at any time within six years of the date on which the competition begins, who has never received any consideration for playing in a match or for giving lessons in the game, and who for a period of five years, prior to first September 1866, has never received a money prize in any Open Competition."

In 1893 a dispute arose regarding the playing of golf on Gullane Common. This was to have wide repercussions for Luffness Golf Club. Unfortunately, when laying out the course in 1867 not all the holes were on Luffness Estate, some being on Gullane Common. The Common extended westwards from Luffness House towards the eastern boundary of Aberlady Bay, north towards Gullane Point then eastwards, skirting the village of Gullane. The dispute centred on a proposal by Mrs Hamilton Ogilvy that Luffness Golf Club should lease from her the right to play golf over that portion of Luffness G.C. course that lay on Gullane Common. At a Club Meeting in January 1894 a proposed agreement between the Club and Mrs Hamilton Ogilvy was discussed when Mr Hope asked that his dissent be recorded on the grounds that Mrs Hamilton Ogilvy had no right to prohibit the Club or any individual member from golfing on Gullane Common. He also objected to any negotiations taking place with her legal agents. At a Club meeting two months later an agreement with Mrs Hamilton Ogilvy was approved, despite an amending motion by a Mr Reid that the meeting be adjourned in order that matters could be further discussed with Mr Hope. It is thought possible that this Mr

Reid was the James Reid who was one of the three people who approached Mr Hope in the latter half of 1894 with a view to forming Luffness **New** Golf Club.

The following extracts from a letter dated 27 January 1894 addressed by Mr Hope's agents to Luffness Golf Club are apposite:

"We are instructed by Mr Hope of Luffness to write you with reference to the proposal on the part of Mrs Hamilton Ogilvy that the club should lease from her the right of playing over that portion of the present golf course situated on Gullane Common. Mr Hope is unable in the interests of himself and of his successors to acquiesce in any arrangement under which part of the golf course on his ground would be leased along with part of a course on the adjoining ground, keeping in view the fact that he has more than sufficient available ground immediately adjoining upon his own estate suitable for making a good golf course. As long as the ground to which Mrs Hamilton Ogilvy has now put forward a claim was admitted to be "common", matters stood upon a different footing. Mr Hope has no desire but to act in the most friendly spirit towards the Luffness Golf Club, and it has occurred to him that a suitable solution of any difficulty that might arise through the claim now put forward by the proprietor of Archerfield would be for the club to abandon the holes on the Gullane Common and to arrange with him for a complete course being formed by combining the new Luffness Mill course with the part of the present Luffness golf course which is situated upon Luffness Links. If an arrangement of the nature indicated by Mr Hope were to be entertained, he thinks it is fitting in the interests of the club and of himself that it should be come to with as little delay as possible, so that the club might profit as much as possible by the expenditure which Mr Hope has already made upon the new course. As you are doubtless aware, this course has been laid out and the putting greens formed, and practically all that is now wanted to bring it into thoroughly good condition is that it should be played over while the green is soft, and before the growing season commences.

Mr Hope's idea is that the present lease held by the club from him should be renounced, and that a new lease should be granted by him of the re-arranged course commencing at Whitsunday first. The conditions of the new lease, which might be say for twelve years, would be very much the same as those contained in the existing lease. A fresh condition, however, would be that the club should be allowed to use the present clubhouse for a period of say three years, as well as getting the use for the same period of the hut on the new course near the Aberlady and Gullane road. By the end of these three years, however, the present clubhouse and hut would revert to Mr Hope, and the club would be taken bound to erect a new clubhouse for themselves at a point near to the corner of the links at the road close to Luffness Mill. . . . If it should be that the club do not see their way to receive favourably the proposals which we now submit to you, Mr Hope desires us to state that at the end of the present lease, which expires in about four and a half years, he would not be prepared to renew it, and that he would make such other arrangements as would seem to him most fitting in the circumstances, . . . and it is his intention if his proposals be rejected to enter into immediate negotiations in regard to the New Luffness Mill course, but of course any new tenants would not get the benefit of that part of the present course on the Luffness Links until the expiry of the existing lease. . . .''

The suggestion made in the foregoing letter that Luffness Golf Club should abandon the holes on Gullane Common and combine the holes on Luffness Links with the recently created Luffness Mill course, was not carried out.

With regard to Luffness Mill course, this was of 18 holes laid out in 1892 by Mr Hope in conjunction with Mr Tom Morris of St Andrews and was ready for play in the spring of 1893. One may wonder at the need for a second course at Luffness but Mr Hope was devoted to the game of golf and was always anxious that the villagers of Aberlady were able to enjoy the game. He also had a vision of creating a golfing centre near Luffness Mill together with a first-class hotel especially for golfers. His original intention was to retain the management of the Luffness Mill course in his own hands but, following an approach by Messrs W. T. Armour, J. Reid and A. M. Ross, he granted them a lease of Luffness Mill course for a period of twelve years with a view to forming a club. This club was Luffness New Golf Club which was formally constituted on 31 October 1894.

With their lease of part of Luffness Estate due to expire in November 1898, Luffness Golf Club approached Mr Hope with the idea of increasing their number of holes on his property to 18 thereby making an 18 hole course on his land. If not successful, the Club would then approach Mrs Hamilton Ogilvy to see if they could have an 18 hole course on Gullane Common. The approach to Mr Hope was made in August 1897 and was broadly similar to the idea originally put forward by him in early 1894, but not carried out. The 1897 approach to Mr Hope was not favourably received by him. In any case, by this time he had already leased the Luffness Mill course to Luffness New Golf Club in 1894. There was also disagreement regarding the possible claim of a right of way over part of Mr Hope's property. Any claim would be resisted by him. There was another factor in that Mr Hope considered that the course required a spell of rest and treatment. In the end he decided not to renew the lease to Luffness Golf Club after expiry at Martinmas 1898.

Mr Hope was always mindful of the needs of Aberlady folk and suggested to Luffness Golf Club that before they committed themselves to the proposal to transfer the Club to Gullane Common, they should remember the excellent piece of golfing ground between Craigielaw farm and the sea. This area is to the west of Aberlady Bay and Mr Hope also reminded them that Aberlady folk had played golf there long before he laid out the Luffness Golf Club course in 1867. Mr Hope was of the view that if asked, Lord Wemyss, a member of Luffness Golf Club, a keen supporter of the game and who had already done so much for Aberlady, would help the villagers of Aberlady by letting them have a course on the land belonging to him at Craigielaw. Lord Wemyss subsequently offered Luffness Golf Club the lease of land at Craigielaw. A course was laid out and inaugurated in November 1898. Thus Luffness Golf Club gave up the 1867 Luffness Links/Gullane Common course and established themselves at Craigielaw. At the Annual General Meeting of Luffness Golf Club held in the Clubhouse, Craigielaw Links, on 30 September 1899, the Club approved the change of their name to The Kilspindie Golf Club.

During the period 1894 to 1898 Luffness Golf Club and Luffness New Golf Club played in close proximity to each other and were frequently referred to as "Old Luffness" and "New Luffness" respectively. After Luffness Golf Club moved across to Craigielaw towards the end of 1898 these descriptions were still in common use and did not really cease until the change of name from Luffness Golf Club to Kilspindie Golf Club. Although Luffness Golf Club and Luffness New Golf Club were entirely separate clubs they had certain similarities, viz: (1) both had "Luffness" in their title; (2) both courses were laid out by Henry Walter Hope of Luffness who was landlord of both clubs in their early years; (3) part of "Old Luffness" course was on Mr Hope's Luffness Estate whilst all of the "New Luffness" course was on Luffness Estate, the courses being in part contiguous.

The clubhouse, 1st tee and 18th green of "Old Luffness" just across the Peffer Bridge, were on Mr Hope's land. In all, eight holes of "Old Luffness" plus portions of ground lying between several holes were on Luffness Estate. These lay west of a line drawn approximately from the present 9th green down through the 14th and 16th greens and 17th tee of Luffness New course. The disputed holes on "Old Luffness" were those on Gullane Common and included the ones along the eastern shore of Aberlady Bay towards Jova's Neuk and Gullane Point. Some of these holes were eventually incorporated into what is now Gullane No. 2 golf course.

Reverting to Luffness Mill course laid out in 1892 and leased by Luffness New Golf Club from 1894, the area it covered is incorporated in today's course. After 1898 some of the land of the "Old Luffness" course was taken over, mainly in the vicinity of today's 14th/15th/16th holes. The remainder of the "Old Luffness" course on Luffness Estate was later put to agricultural use. The first three holes of the Mill course were much as they are today. There was the famous Hill hole across the quarry at Gala Law, then hole no. 5. The 6th was today's 7th hole with the green perched high on Gullane Hill. The 9th, 10th, 11th, 17th and 18th holes were somewhat similar to today. Many changes have of course since been made over the years.

When the approach was made to Mr Hope in 1894 to lease the Luffness Mill course and form a club it is thought that there was a long waiting list for membership of Luffness Golf Club ("Old Luffness"). The founding members of Luffness New Golf Club numbered about 100 and it is possible that some of them had been on this waiting list. These founding members each paid six pounds for life membership whilst for others the entrance fee was fixed at three guineas with an annual subscription of one guinea.

The Club was formally inaugurated at a meeting held on 31 October 1894 at Dowell's Rooms, Edinburgh, when the first office-bearers were elected. These were:

President — Henry Walter Hope of Luffness
Captain — The Right Honourable Lord Leconfield
Secretary — James Reid
Trustees — Lord Kingsburgh; Lord Trayner; W. G. Bloxsom; W. T. Armour; A. Mackenzie Ross; James Reid

Eighty-five years later, on purchasing the course, the Club became a Limited Company of which the first Directors were:

Donald Ross Sandison, Edinburgh   (Captain)
Hamish Sidney Urquhart Steven, Chirnside   (Vice-Captain)
James Christie Falconer, Gullane   (Secretary)
Michael John Bell, Inveresk
Gerald George Kirkby, North Berwick
David Ruthven Lawrie, Edinburgh
Alasdair David Macintyre, Edinburgh
Michael Douglas Mayer, Edinburgh
David Mathieson Miller, Edinburgh

The story of Luffness New Golf Club continues taking each decade in turn:

1894-1903

There is no official record of the formation of the Club as the Minute Books No. 1 and No. 2 for the period 1894 to January 1927 have been lost. This loss, discovered in 1949, constitutes a serious gap in our knowledge of the first thirty-three years of the history of the Club. Fortunately there are abstracts of Club accounts and some sundry papers covering these years.

On 11 October 1894 a professional tournament was held to mark the formal opening of the course. Those invited to compete for money prizes were: Willie Auchterlonie (Open Champion 1893), Andrew Kirkcaldy, Tom Morris (all of St Andrews); David Grant, Ben Sayers, G. Sayers, P. Wynne (all of North Berwick); J. Simpson (Edinburgh); B. Campbell (Musselburgh); G. Shepherd ("Old Luffness"); E. Fitzjohn (Muirfield); H. Gillane (Gullane). The tournament was won by Ben Sayers with a score of 166 for 36 holes.

The first Club competition took place on 23 April 1895 when F. G. Tait won the award for the best scratch score with a round of 76. The award was the Leconfield Gold Medal presented by the Captain, the Right Honourable Lord Leconfield. The score of 76 set a new course record beating the previous record of 82 held by Ben Sayers of North Berwick. With the score of 76 plus 4 = net 80 F. G.(Freddie) Tait also won the prize for the best handicap score. This prize was a Silver Quaich presented by Messrs W. T. Armour and J. Reid.

The second meeting was held in October 1895 when F. G. Tait again won the prize for the best scratch score, the Hope Medal presented by the Club President, Mr Henry Walter Hope of Luffness. The Ross Medal presented by A. M. Ross for the best handicap score was won by W. T. Armour with a round of 89 less 4 to give a net 85.

The Accounts for the first year to 10 November 1895 show that 98 Original (Life) members had paid their dues but that three had not yet done so. There is no complete Club record of Foundation members but amongst that distinguished number is the name of the Right Honourable A. J. Balfour (later Earl Balfour, K.G.), Prime Minister 1902-05. During that first year 98 Ordinary members were admitted.

The original clubhouse was a small wooden building located not far from the present greenkeepers' "bothy". Each member had a key to the door and a few lockers, or boxes as they were then known, were available for rental at 5/- per annum or a single payment of £1 5/-. Towards the end of 1895 work started on a new clubhouse on the same site as the existing clubhouse. The Specification & Schedule of Measurements for the new building shows:

Carpenter & Joiner & Glazing Work	...	...	£334 8 4d
Mason & Brick Works	...	...	£297 15 2d
Tiler Work	...	...	£133 12 6d
Plumber Work	...	...	£100 1 5d

The formal opening of the new Clubhouse took place on 3 April 1896.

A major event in 1898 was the winning of the East Lothian County Cup when the Club was represented by F. G. Tait, W. T. Armour, A. M. Ross and T. T. Gray. This Competition was inaugurated in 1871 when the Earl of Wemyss presented a Silver Challenge Bowl to Luffness Golf Club for annual competition between East Lothian Clubs. The following participated in 1898: Bass Rock, Dirleton Castle, Gullane, Haddington, Honourable Company of Edinburgh Golfers, Luffness, Luffness New, New Club North Berwick, Thorntree. Notable absentees were Archerfield and Dunbar. Luffness New had wins over Dirleton Castle and the Honourable Company of Edinburgh Golfers and beat Tantallon in the final. 1898 marked the the end of an era in that this was the last occasion on which this competition was played over the old Luffness Links (Luffness Golf Club), i.e., the links course laid out in 1867 on Luffness Estate/Gullane Common.

The 1899 edition of the Club Rules & Regulations is the earliest held. The following are three extracts:

1. The name of the Club shall be "LUFFNESS NEW GOLF CLUB".

2. The Club shall consist of six hundred and fifty members. Officers of the Army on the Staff, or in Garrison in Edinburgh and district, and Officers of the Royal Navy on duty on the local coast, shall, during the period of their official residence respectively, be eligible as extraordinary Members, and enjoy all the privileges of the Club on payment of the Annual Subscription, the year for which such payment is made to run from the date of payment.

3. The Rules of Golf, as they may from time to time be fixed by the Royal and Ancient Golf Club, St Andrews, shall, so far as applicable, and with such special additions as may be made by the Committee, be the Rules of Golf for this Club.

In the early years there is frequent reference in the Accounts to payments to Miss Scott, a draper, for wool for the flags whilst the 1895 Accounts show the purchase from Miss Thomson of a cart, horse and harness at a total of £7 7/-. Shoeing of the horse was an additional 3/4d.

Mr Henry Walter Hope of Luffness, President of the Club and also the landlord, took a very keen interest in the course and in 1899 arranged for Mr Tom Morris to visit Luffness New. A large programme of work was discussed and carried out in the ensuing months. Nearly every teeing ground was re-sited or altered in some way, bunkers were remodelled or repaired and much work was carried out on the greens. Several fairways were heavily sanded and rolled, whilst a chain harrow was used over the extensive areas of very rough ground.

Miss Ellen Louisa Purcell was appointed Clubmistress in 1901 at an annual salary of £18 18/-. The Accounts show payments of this amount to her for the next six years but there is no record of when she ceased to be employed by the Club. Her brother, Mr H. Purcell, was owner of the Golf Hotel, Aberlady, and supplied food and liquor to the Club. At this time whisky was sold to members for 4/6d a bottle or 6d per glass whilst, on being given a day's notice, Miss Purcell provided luncheons at 2/6d per head.

In September 1903 a private railway platform was opened at Luffness for the sole use of members of the Club. It was on the line built by the Aberlady, Gullane and North Berwick Railway Company and opened as far as Gullane in 1898. The proposed extension to North Berwick was never built. The line branched off the main Edinburgh – Berwick-upon-Tweed line of the North British Railway Company at Spittal about 1½ miles east of Longniddry. Prior to the opening of the Gullane line the members used to alight at Longniddry Railway Station and travel to Luffness by horse-drawn wagonette. For the Spring and Autumn Meetings the Club reserved special compartments on the trains from Edinburgh and starting

Luffness Halt, adjacent to 2nd fairway.
Courtesy of Jackson Collection: Glasgow University Archives

Ladies and caddies at Luffness New G.C. (Alex Glasgow's daughters)

times were linked to the arrival of the trains. The increased use of motor-cars rendered the Luffness Platform redundant and it was removed in 1931. The line to Gullane was closed for passenger traffic a year later.

What else was happening in this decade:

1895 — Sir Henry Wood founded the Promenade Concerts.

1897 — The first conviction took place of a motorist, for drunken driving.

1901 — The first Royal Navy submarine was launched.

1904-1913

The Accounts tell us that in 1906 the hire of Dowell's Rooms in Edinburgh for a meeting was five shillings and that in the following year the Club paid £2 10/- to a Mr Pattison for boots for the horse. Each year the Accounts show ''wages for the green'' but the names of the greenstaff are not given.

The 1909 edition of the Club Rules and Regulations contain the following three bye-laws:

1. In the event of Guests who are introduced in terms of Rule 13 playing over the Course, they shall each pay to the greenkeeper or Club Mistress, who will supply the necessary tickets, One Shilling per day of Green Money, for which payments introducing Members shall be responsible.
2. The Committee shall have power to provide for the election, as temporary Members, of Strangers resident for the time being in the District, and Members of other Golf Clubs, on such terms as the Committee shall fix.
3. Ladies shall **not** be admitted to the Club House.

(Bye-law No. 3 was still in force in 1917 and it is not known when it was amended to admit ladies within the precincts of the clubhouse, albeit restricted to a ladies' room!)

Perhaps the most important event in this decade was the renewal of the Club lease in 1911. This was granted for a period of 21 years, but only after lengthy negotiations had taken place. One of the conditions in the 1911 lease was that Sunday golf was not permitted without the written consent of the landlord. This was eventually given in 1922 but only on condition that no caddies or labour of any description were employed on a Sunday. Another condition was that a properly qualified greenkeeper should be employed and that he be in attendance daily.

One of the items **not** agreed during negotiations was the landlord's wish that a working-men's club be formed with the right to play over the course on payment of a nominal subscription, but without right to the use of the clubhouse. The Club Committee were of the opinion that should any artisans' club be formed in Aberlady and district, the Club would give the fullest consideration to any proposals for them playing over the course but all control would have to be vested in Luffness New Golf Club.

In the Accounts for 1912-13 there is reference for the first time to a payment of £55 for the Clubmaster's annual salary. No name is given but from later records it is known that Mr Alexander Lockhart Glasgow of Aberlady was appointed in 1912 as the first resident Clubmaster, a position he held with great distinction until his death in 1938. In a later report there is mention of him having been associated with the Club since 1900 but it is not clear in what capacity.

In 1912 plans were prepared by Messrs Cooper & Taylor, Architects, Edinburgh, for alterations and additions to the clubhouse. These included the addition of a dining room, ladies' room, drying room and accommodation for a clubmaster, also alterations and improvements to the kitchen and lavatory. The cost was £1,592 17/3d. This was financed by a transfer from the surplus Club revenue, donations of £101 18/- and the issue of £750 worth of debentures. These were in multiples of £50 and carried interest at 4½% per annum less income tax, payable annually on 11 November. It was expected that repayment would be made within the period of the lease which was due to expire at Martinmas 1932.

Tailpiece:

    1907 — Dinizulu, King of the Zulus, surrendered; the rebellion had been triggered off by the imposition of a poll tax.

    1912 — 96 were arrested after a suffragette raid on the House of Commons.

    1913 — D. H. Lawrence published *Sons and Lovers*.

1914-1923

The Great War dominated the lives of many during this decade, not only during the war years but also in the aftermath which included a period of industrial unrest. In September 1914 it was decided to cancel the Autumn Meeting scheduled for the following month and at the Annual General Meeting in March 1915 it was resolved that Club competitions be meantime abandoned.

The financial position at November 1916 revealed a deficiency of £96 12/10d and at the AGM in March of the next year it was decided to deal with this by raising a levy of £1 per member. It was noted that 65 members were serving in HM Forces and that the majority were loyally supporting the Club by paying their subscriptions even though they had no chance of using the Club. Nonetheless it was hoped that they too would pay the levy of £1!

Club competitions resumed in 1919. At that time there were three ballots for play, one for play starting at 9 a.m., the second on the arrival of the 9.35 a.m. train from Edinburgh and the third on the arrival of the 1.35 p.m. from Edinburgh. Reports of Club competitions received lengthy coverage in the Edinburgh and local press. The following brief extract from a press report of the Autumn Meeting in 1920 is an example of the style of reporting:

"The grand score of 73 was registered by Mr W. B. Torrance who was in his happiest scoring mood. In the out half his all-round play was practically free from fault, his short game being of deadly character, and this portion including as many as four 3s . . . his card of 73, proved winner of the Scratch trophy. Mr A. W. Duncan, who was round in 76, was bunkered at the third and sixth holes, but, despite this, he succeeded in turning at 37. A 6 at the eleventh hole was the result of his taking three putts, and at the sixteenth he was robbed of a 3 by the same course."

During this decade it seems appropriate to note the service given to the Club by Mr J. A. Robertson-Durham. He was elected Captain in 1914, carried on in that capacity until April 1921 when he continued for a further two years as a Committee Member.

In 1921 the following Notice was sent to Life Members:

"It has been suggested that the Life Members who have for so many years enjoyed the privileges of the Club in respect of their original contribution of £6 should be given an opportunity of making a donation to the Club's Funds. The Committee hope you will see your way to subscribe."

It is not clear what the response was.

In 1922 plans were approved for alterations to the clubhouse at an estimated cost of £1,200. These included enlarging the kitchen and service accommodation, conversion of the existing ladies' room into additional apartments for the Clubmaster, and on the ground floor adjoining what was then referred to as the "Lunch Room", the provision of a new room for ladies.

In November of that year it was decided to open the course and clubhouse on a Sunday. This had repercussions three years later when the Club received a "Protest and Appeal" deploring the playing of golf on a Sunday and appealing for such play to be discontinued. This Protest was signed on behalf of: the Church of Scotland; United Free Church of Scotland; Free Church of Scotland; United Original Secession Church of Scotland; Reformed Presbyterian Church of Scotland; Congregational Union of Scotland; Baptist Union of Scotland; Synod, Primitive Methodist Church; Scotland Synod, Wesleyan Methodist Church. There is no record of a reply to this overture and Sunday play continued.

Tailpiece:

1915 — The Military Cross was introduced and the first award made on 1 January.
1920 — Sir William Robertson became the only private soldier to attain the rank of Field Marshal.
1923 — Jack Hobbs scored his 100th century in first class cricket.

What better way to start the story of this decade than to quote from a newspaper report of 26 April 1924 regarding the Spring Meeting:

"... All these returns were eventually dwarfed by the outstanding performance of Mr W. B. Torrance, who surely never played better golf, and possibly never quite equalled his mechanical like perfection of Saturday, and who broke the record of the green by as many as five strokes, with his great score of 67. Although putting well, it was not to this department of the game, that his exceptional card was due, as he got down only one long putt, holing out from about six yards at the sixth; but his wooden play, both from the tee and through the course, was of the brilliant order, getting away long shots well on the line, and being so deadly with his seconds that he left himself little to do on the green. His great score of 31 outward included no fewer than five actual threes...."

Over 100 played in that Meeting and of the leading handicap scores, three had handicaps of plus 3; three of plus 2; one of plus 1; nine were scratch whilst seventeen had handicaps ranging from 1 to 9.

In September 1924 James Braid submitted a Report on his suggested changes to the course. This Report took into account the possibility that one day the Club might be prevented from playing across the public road, Aberlady/Gullane (A198). In order to get a picture of what the course was like then compared with the present day it might be helpful to note:

Holes no. 1, 2 and 3 were more or less as they are today. Hole no. 4 was played from near to the present 4th tee, across the road to a green on the eastern side of the quarry. At that time the Quarry Hole was the 5th hole. The 12th and 13th holes were much as they are today having been re-sited in 1910/1911, prior to which time they had been played across the main road.

In his Report Mr Braid suggested that a new 4th hole be made, viz:

"Dogleg towards Clubhouse, using part of the present fairway for tee shot. This hole would be played over good land, which would only require cutting and rolling (very few rabbit scrapes) on to green near foot path, keep green nearly natural contour, strip turf off present 18th east of road and put back turf stripped off position for green."

A new no. 5 hole was also suggested, viz:

"Tee close to 1st tee and played on to green short of road and east thereof nearly in line with present 5th tee (original tee of Quarry Hole), strip turf from 4th fairway to return this green, putting back the turf lifted from position of green."

The Quarry Hole, then hole 5, would become hole 6 with the teeing ground continuing to be east of the quarry, i.e. play across the quarry. James Braid suggested various alterations to some of the tees and bunkers but the other main alteration was to the 18th hole where he proposed:

> "Tee about 80 yards behind present back tee and to the south of green, making hole about 450 yards on to a green just short of road, strip turf from position marked and keep undulating, relay best of the turf, balance required to be taken east of the road, fill in one bunker and make six others, positions pointed out on spot."

All suggestions were carried out and the new layout was ready for play in the spring of 1925.

Over the next few years a considerable amount of work was done on the construction of new greens, tees and bunkers whilst in 1932 the 10th green was re-sited as it was considered to be too near the 9th fairway.

At the Spring Meeting in 1925 the gradual change in transport facilities was evident in that when replying to the ballot, members were asked to indicate if they were travelling by train or motor. In that year matches were played against the Oxford and Cambridge Golfing Society, the Royal Aberdeen Golf Club and the Royal Liverpool Golf Club.

In 1927 six girls were employed for weeding of the greens during winter and the following year there is a report of two of the girls found asleep on the 9th green. History does not relate what disciplinary measures, if any, were taken – they must have been very tired!?

In 1928 a house was built for the Head Greenkeeper who hitherto had lived in Aberlady. This house has since been added to and improved and is currently occupied by the Head Greenkeeper.

Mr Gault, the Head Greenkeeper, resigned in 1929 having obtained a position in France and in his place Mr Thomas Martin of St Andrews was appointed. Another change that year was the death of the Club Secretary, Mr G. C. Manford, who was succeeded in office by Mr J. D. Lownie.

In 1931 plans were approved for a new garage, tool shed and caddie shelter. This was one building of brick, harled and tiled to match the clubhouse. In 1932 the Committee considered an estimate for the installation of electricity in the Clubhouse but decided not to take any action.

Up to now the scratch and handicap trophy winners at the Spring and Autumn Meetings had been given bronze charms and in 1933 it was resolved that in future they should be of gold. A supply was purchased at a cost of £1 each.

Tailpiece:

1928 — The voting age for women was reduced from 30 to 21.
1931 — Third-party insurance for motorists became compulsory.
1933 — The first "photograph" of the Loch Ness Monster was published.

1934-1943

In January 1934, following the severe droughts of 1932 and 1933 when the greens became almost unplayable, it was decided to investigate a system of piping water to each green. At first it was thought that water from Brand's Well, near to the 7th green, could be used. This water was analysed and found to be satisfactory, but as it would have been necessary to build a large storage tank as well as laying piping to all greens, the idea was abandoned on the grounds of expense. Brand's Well is a flat-topped stone structure about 2m × 1m × 1m and has for some years been almost completely dry. It is thought that it might have been a 12th-century Holy Well. It gave an abundant supply of water and up to the end of the 19th century was used by some of the villagers from Gullane before Gullane obtained a piped water supply. The Club then made application to East Lothian County Council for permission to make 1 inch connections to the main 7 inch pipe from the Lammermuir Hills to Gullane which passed through the centre of the course. This was granted and the project was completed in the summer of 1934 by Andrew Mann, Plumber, Gullane.

The following are two excerpts from press reports on the visit in April of the Oxford and Cambridge Golfing Society:

> The Scotsman's Special Representative wrote: "The Oxford and Cambridge Golfing Society's touring team, which includes Cyril Tolley and Roger Wethered who will take up duty again in the British side for the Walker Cup match next month, played the first of their three engagements in East Lothian yesterday, when they met a side representing the Luffness New Golf Club. . . . The Oxford and Cambridge party winning over the day by 9½ matches to 6½. The Luffness course, with medal tees in commission, presented a stiff test, made stiffer still by the weather conditions. The Club are having water laid on their course following the scare they naturally underwent about their greens after the drought of last summer."

> The Golf Correspondent of The Times, Bernard Darwin, wrote: ". . . Luffness was the battlefield. I had not seen it since it had been altered owing to the traffic on the road, and I felt a little lost, but there was all the old charm of peace and solitude and the most perfect turf on which the human foot ever trod. Some of the greens had suffered a little in the drought, but they had all the old pleasant pace, and there remains the old blind hole over the quarry. By no stretch of the imagination can it be called a good hole, but one feels a sentimental attachment for it, especially if by some gorgeous fluke the ball lands near the hole."

In 1935 further improvements to the clubhouse were approved, including an extension to the smoke-room and the dining room at a cost of £1,358 14 9d. Electricity was installed in the Clubhouse.

1936 saw the introduction of Five Day Membership, i.e., those who were not permitted to play on Saturdays and Sundays. Also in 1936, the landlord gave permission for caddies to be employed on a Sunday provided they were over the age of 18 years.

In 1937, the Head Greenkeeper, Thomas Martin, resigned to take up an appointment at Coombe Hill Golf Club, London, and was succeeded by James King, formerly an Assistant Greenkeeper at Gullane Golf Club.

Members were greatly saddened by the death on 4 December 1938 of Mr Alexander Lockhart Glasgow, at the age of 63. He had been associated with the Club since 1900 and in 1912 became the first Resident Clubmaster. He was well known throughout the golfing world and referred to affectionately as "Alex". He was a native of Aberlady where he was an elder of the Parish Church. For some time he had been Secretary of the Aberlady Unionist Association and Secretary of Aberlady Rifle Club.

In December 1938 Mr Glasgow's daughter and son-in-law, Mr and Mrs William Gilchrist, were appointed Joint Clubmaster and Clubmistress and took up their positions in February 1939.

Mr Gilchrist was unsuccessful in an application for a commission as a Catering Officer in the Royal Air Force and subsequently, in 1942, received a temporary post with the Scottish Motor Traction Co. Ltd. He was, however, free on Saturday afternoons and Sundays and able to assist his wife with clubhouse duties.

Mr King, Head Greenkeeper, joined the Royal Observer Corps but was able to give his services to the Club in his spare time. Later in 1942, following retirement due to ill-health of greenkeeper William Clark, two boys were appointed to the greenstaff, who, together with Mr King, on a part-time basis, kept the work going until the end of the war.

Tailpiece:

1934 — The "Flying Scotsman" reached a speed of 97 m.p.h.
1936 — The *Queen Mary* sailed on her maiden voyage.
1938 — Scotland Yard decided on the use of police dogs.

1944-1953

The 50th Jubilee Year of the Club was 1944 but in view of the conditions then existing, no celebrations were held.

During the war years the course was frequently used for military exercises when the greens would be roped off. Fortunately no serious damage was done to the fairways. Although staff conditions presented difficulties, the course continued to be in good playing order throughout the war whilst the clubhouse staff coped well with the many catering restrictions imposed upon them.

In May 1945 Mr and Mrs Gilchrist resigned as Clubmaster and Clubmistress to start a private hotel in Gullane. To replace them, Mr Peter I. Jamieson from Galashiels was appointed Clubmaster with Mrs Jamieson as Cook.

Mr James King was released in May 1945 from service in the Royal Observer Corps. Later that year, Mr Alexander Thomson, a former member of staff, was appointed to the greenstaff. He was subsequently to become Head Geeenkeeper in 1970. Within another twelve months the greenstaff complement was restored to its pre-war level of five.

At the AGM in 1947 Dr A. Cleland demitted office as Captain after holding that office for the unprecedented period of nine years.

In July 1947 the whisky ration for the Club was 20 bottles per month of which two were sold on Saturdays, two on Sundays and one bottle or less, for the remaining days of the week.

In 1948 a proposal that the greens be swept on Sundays was rejected by the Committee on the grounds that the extra cost of two men at 7/6d each was not justified. A similar proposal in 1949 was also turned down for the same reason, but eventually approved in 1950 following an entry in the Suggestion Book signed by 24 members!

Towards the end of 1948 Mr J. D. Lownie, Secretary, intimated his wish to demit office and in the summer of the following year Mr W. H. Stevenson was appointed in his place.

In February 1949 at the suggestion of the retiring Captain, Mr James Cooper, it was decided to hold a Summer Meeting in addition to the Spring and Autumn Meetings. The first Summer Meeting was held on 16 July that year when Mr Cooper donated a Cup for the best handicap score. The Trayner Cup (Competition for Bogey and Handicap), which had not been played for since 1912, was awarded for the best scratch score at the Summer Meetings.

The trapping and sale of rabbits provided a useful source of income for the Club and in 1949, Mr Alex Thomson, a member of the greenstaff and a former trapper, was deployed to do six months' greenkeeping and six months' rabbit trapping. The controlled price then was 11d per pound and the rabbits were sold to Messrs George Campbell & Son, Game Dealers, Edinburgh, who called at the course regularly to collect them.

In December 1949 it was decided that the war-time anti-tank concrete blocks at the rear of the 18th green interfered with play and made the back of the green difficult to see. To rectify the matter a bank of earth was built up against and in the spaces between the blocks whilst the blocks were turfed over with rough grass.

In the summer of 1949 Mr Robin Wight, a member and a scratch player, won the Scottish Amateur Championship at Muirfield. Another, but quite different happening that summer was the request by the Lothians Agricultural Committee that arrangements be made for the grazing of sheep on the course. These were made and grazing continued for several years.

At the Annual General Meeting in 1950 Mr J. D. Lownie, the recently retired Secretary of the Club, was made the first Honorary Member. This honour has since been bestowed on several eminent and worthy members but only two other Secretaries have received it, namely W. H. (Billy) Stevenson in 1967 and James Falconer in 1984.

The highlight of 1951 was the winning of the East Lothian County Cup when the Club was represented by R. Wight, A. W. Small, T. C. Scott and J. R. Ness. This was only the second time the Club had been successful in this competition, the first being in 1898.

East Lothian County Cup Winners, 1951

R. Wight and A. W. Small,   *T. C. Scott and J. R. Ness,*
First Couple   *Second Couple*

At the 1951 AGM a proposal was made that the name of the Club be changed to Luffness Golf Club. The Committee were in approval and sought permission of the Club President who was also the landlord. This was granted, but the President recommended that the views of Kilspindie Golf Club be sought to see if they had any objection. They did object, and on two grounds, firstly that when the split occurred in Luffness Golf Club those who went to the present Kilspindie course retained the name and it was not until later that the name was changed to the Kilspindie Golf Club, secondly, the name, Luffness Golf Club, still appeared on many of their trophies. Later in the year the Captain and Secretary met their counterparts at

Kilspindie Golf Club and in the course of the discussion it appeared that there was some objection to the change as between the landlords of the two Clubs. The Committee deemed it advisable not to press the matter further.

In October 1952 a request was made for an alternative tee at the 6th (Quarry Hole) to obviate the necessity of elderly members having to climb the hill to the existing tee. A golf architect, Mr Mackenzie Ross, was consulted, and in January 1953 work started on a second optional tee. At the 1954 AGM it was decided that this alternative tee should become the official tee. One member dissented as he considered the Quarry Hole was a feature of the course and should be left as it was. It is not known why stone was quarried at Gala Law. The most likely explanation seems to be that the stone was used in the construction of the main road between Aberlady and Gullane.

Towards the end of 1952 a suggestion was made that a Winter Foursomes Competition be held and at the AGM in the following year the retiring Captain, Mr John S. Wells, presented a Silver Bowl as a trophy for this competition.

Up to now it had been the custom for the retiring Captain to make a recommendation to the Committee regarding his successor but since the 1953 AGM the new Captain has been elected following a recommendation made by a Sub-Committee consisting of the Captain and Past-Captains.

In November 1953 the bar measures were changed from ¼ gill to ⅕ gill. This was followed by the introduction of an unofficial "Luffness measure" of ⅖ gill. Unless a member has indicated otherwise a request for spirits is responded to by the measure of ⅖ gill.

Tailpiece:

> 1946 — William Joyce ("Lord Haw Haw") was hanged for treason.
> 1950 — A large consignment of smuggled nylon stockings was discovered on board the liner *Franconia* at Liverpool.
> 1952 — Identity cards were abolished.

1954-1963

1954 saw the introduction of Country Membership and Junior Membership. Later that year in October there were the first reports of myxomatosis making it difficult to find a market for the rabbits! On the last day of the year the death occurred of the Clubmaster, Mr P. I. Jamieson. He was succeeded in the spring of 1955 by Mr J. N. Gourlay.

Family Tickets were introduced in March 1955 and sold in books of eight tickets for £1. Another event that year was the inauguration of Club Dinners, the first being held on 22 October in the Royal British

Hotel, Edinburgh, with Mr T. C. Scott as Recorder. The first Dinner to be held in the Clubhouse was in May 1957 but thereafter Edinburgh continued as the venue for some years. Dinners are currently held in the Clubhouse four times a year usually in January, March, June and October – black tie obligatory.

In 1956 an area south of the 4th fairway was designated as a practice ground and a practice putting green was re-established near the Clubhouse. It might be thought that by now, war-time restrictions would have been forgotten about but, at the end of the year, petrol rationing was still in force.

In 1957 a proposal was again made that a Club Tie be introduced but again turned down. More importantly that year, a suggestion was made at a Committee Meeting that the Club should endeavour to purchase the course. A tentative figure of £7,000 was mooted on the basis of a 5% yield of the rent. The proposal was remitted to the Past Captains who gave their approval for an informal approach to be made to the landlord's agents. The approach was not successful.

In May 1958 permission was given to one member to ride a bicycle on the course otherwise he would have been unable to play! It is not known if permission was for one day only or for all subsequent days. The first Caddiemaster was appointed. For several years there had been a request for such a post, but all had been turned down on the grounds of expense. The retirement of Mr William Cunningham from the greenstaff seemed an appropriate moment and he was appointed for duty on Saturdays and Sundays at the rate of £2 per week in addition to his Club pension of £1 weekly.

Members may have noticed a small African Drum in the Trophy Cabinet and wondered where it came from. This was a gift to the Club following a match in June 1962 with the Uganda Golfing Society who were on a brief tour of courses in Scotland.

In March 1963 the concrete blocks, war-time anti-tank obstacles, were removed from alongside the 12th fairway and used in the construction of Cockenzie Power Station. In May a match against Gullane Golf Club was held and this later became an annual event. In addition that year it was decided to accept a gift of "The 1892 Cup" and to award it as a trophy for the best aggregate scratch scores out of the Spring, Summer and Autumn Meetings. The donor was Mr Donald Smith, a member, and the cup had been won by his grandfather, Mr James Smith of Leith, as a Handicap Prize at "Old Luffness" in 1892.

Tailpiece:

1954 — Food rationing ended in Britain.
1959 — The M1 motorway was opened.
1963 — The Royal Navy's first nuclear-powered submarine, *Dreadnought*, was commissioned.

1964-1973

Having previously been declined on several occasions, a request for a drinking tap on the course was agreed and one was installed in 1964 between the 9th green and the 10th tee.

In December 1965 Mr J. N. Gourlay, who had been Clubmaster for the previous ten years, died. His widow carried on his duties and retired in November 1967 when she was succeeded by Mr Jim Scotland with Mrs Scotland being responsible for the catering arrangements. Another change in officials took place that year when Mr W. H. Stevenson demitted office as Secretary and in his stead Mr J. W. Oswald was appointed.

A major happening in 1970 was the retirement of Mr James King, the Head Greenkeeper, who had held that post since 1937. He was a man of great ability and one of the "characters" of the Club. To succeed him the Club appointed the Foreman Greenkeeper, Mr Alexander Thomson.

The first match against a team from Royal St George's Golf Club took place in May 1970. Their team was named "The Barbadians" and the Luffness Captain, having recently returned from a visit to Antigua, named his side "The Antiguans". Also that year, a former Captain of the Club, Mr R. I. Marshall, presented a trophy for competition by the older members. This was the Marshall Quaich awarded for the best handicap score at the Summer Meeting by a member over the age of 60.

In January 1971 the Waiting List for entry to the Club numbered 60 including those who had been elected to membership but had decided to defer entry. Further investigation revealed that the list contained only those who had deferred entry. This was not a very healthy position as it was possible that some who had deferred would never join.

The United East Lothian Pest Control Society was formed in 1971 and the Club became members in the expectation of help in reducing the number of rabbits whose depredations on the course were now of serious proportions.

On 17 October 1971 the Committee agreed that "The custom of prohibiting ladies from wearing trousers in the mixed lounge and dining room should be discontinued".

Because of the large number of members wishing to play in the Spring, Summer and Autumn Meetings it was decided to hold these Meetings over two days with members having the choice of one of two days. This occurred in 1972. In 1971 it was agreed that two competitions, mainly for the younger members, should be held in the summer months. One was held in May 1972 with the second the following month. A check of membership in November 1972 revealed that nearly one quarter of ordinary members were over the age of 65 and only ten under the age of 30!

In March 1972 the Secretary indicated his wish to retire and for the first time it was decided not to restrict applications for the post from solely within the Club membership. Hitherto it had been the custom to appoint a member with a professional office in Edinburgh.

A small Secretary's Office was prepared in the Clubhouse by using part of the locker room. Mr Peter Whyte took up his duties as Secretary and Treasurer in November 1972 but after 6½ months in office felt it necessary to intimate his wish to retire at the end of the financial year. He was succeeded as Secretary and Treasurer in November 1973 by Mr James Falconer, also on a part-time basis, but it became evident within a very short time that the work-load was properly full-time. This was partly due to the transfer to the Secretary of some supervisory jobs previously done by the Clubmaster and Head Greenkeeper but mainly because it seemed that much of the routine secretarial and book-keeping duties had in earlier years been done by staff in the Secretary's own professional office in Edinburgh.

To revert to 1972, by the end of that year much concern was being expressed at the very poor condition of several of the fairways, attributed to the semi-drought conditions of the previous two years. In 1973 intensive spiking of the fairways was undertaken but this was only the start of what was to become, over the next few years, a major programme of work to restore the course to its former excellent state.

At the AGM in 1973 it was decided to investigate once again the possibility of buying the course. It was thought that the price might be in the region of £50,000. Unfortunately, an approach to the landlord revealed that he was still not prepared to sell.

Tailpiece:

1964 — The Forth Road Bridge was opened by the Queen.
1970 — The 10/- note went out of circulation.
1973 — The Open University awarded its first degrees.

1974-1983

The highlights of this period were the restoration of the course from its near catastrophic condition due mainly to the semi-drought in 1971-73 when the average rainfall was 16·88 inches compared with an average of 26·48 inches over the previous ten years; the re-establishment of the Club as a main club for most of the membership plus the need to attract younger members; the purchase of the course in 1979.

The recently appointed Secretary felt an urgent need to identify himself with the work of the greenkeeping staff in their battle to rehabilitate the links and obtained a place on a short course at The Sports Turf Research Institute, Bingley, held mainly for Head Greenkeepers.

In March 1974 the death occurred of the Head Greenkeeper, Mr Alex Thomson, who had been with the Club since 1946. Pending the appointment of a successor, Mr James King, living in retirement in

29

Aberlady, was persuaded to make advisory visits. It is of note that he was the last greenkeeper at Luffness to carry out the lifting of entire greens, i.e., rolling back the turf and lifting off, re-sanding the base and relaying.

In June 1974 the Club was fortunate in obtaining the services of Mr Robert Watt as Head Greenkeeper, a position he had held at Haddington Golf Club. As a native of Gullane and having served his apprenticeship at Gullane Golf Club he was well acquainted with the needs of a seaside links. His leadership and skill played a large part in bringing the course back to the standard expected of a Championship course.

Throughout the long restoration period the advice of Mr J. H. (Jim) Arthur, then the Agronomist to the Championship Committee of the Royal and Ancient Golf Club, was invaluable. The fairways badly affected were 8-11-12-13-14-17-18, and after numerous tests, it was thought that the manurial state of the soil had nothing to do with poor grass cover. The significant difference between the poor and good areas was in the organic content of the soil. The initial remedial measure was to encourage drought resistance and the fairways were heavily spiked then top dressed with granulated sedge peat, with the harrow being used to work the peat well down into the spiked holes. The choice of peat was important and it was obtained from a fairly neutral fen in East Anglia and delivered to Luffness in huge lorries. Basic greenkeeping principles were adhered to—aeration, top dressing, the minimum or even nil use of fertilisers, scarifying of the greens, with just enough watering to keep the grass alive. By many standards the greens were in good shape but by Luffness standards there were a few poor ones, notably 1, 4 and 18. All greens were deep hand hollow-tined to about a depth of 9 inches. The tees, too, received treatment.

Rabbits were a major problem at this time and in the very early morning the 9th fairway was a favourite place to see them in very large numbers. Methods used to combat them were trapping, gassing, ferreting, shooting by day and shooting at night with the aid of car headlights. "Long netting" was about to be tried but fortunately after a few years the numbers receded to such an extent that this was not necessary.

The Club has always had a large membership from Edinburgh and district, averaging roughly 70 per cent of the membership. With the high inflation of the 'seventies many who were members of town and country clubs cut down with a resultant loss to Luffness. Because of a preponderance of older members, strenuous efforts were made to encourage new and preferably younger members to join. These efforts were successful and in 1976 alone, 75 new ordinary members joined. Although the Waiting List was virtually nil throughout this decade, the total membership was maintained near to or at the permitted level. The following table may be of interest:

ORDINARY MEMBERS	JANUARY 1974	SEPTEMBER 1981
Age 75 and over	11	17
Age 65-74	100	87
Age 45-64	265	201
	376	305
Age 35-44	54	97
Age 25-43	27	54
Under 25	2	3
	459	459

Other changes in this decade were the resignation of the Clubmaster, Mr Jim Scotland, in 1974, and the appointment in his stead of Mr Edward Gilligan. His wife Mrs Moira Gilligan who was in charge of catering had made a brave fight against a long illness and died in November 1981. Mr Gilligan carried on with the help of his daughter, but resigned at the end of 1982. He was succeeded by Mr Alan Guthrie with his wife in charge of catering.

In 1974/75 essential improvements were made in the Clubhouse to the staff changing room, staff lavatories, store room and to the ladies' changing room, whilst a third bedroom was added to the Head Greenkeeper's cottage. Sorely needed additions were made to the greenkeeping equipment and an application was submitted to the planning authorities for permission to build a machinery shed cum work shed.

At the AGM in March 1975 the retiring Captain suggested that the Club should have a Captain's Badge of Office. It was considered expedient at that time to use an item in the trophy cabinet for this purpose. This was a medallion inscribed "Luffness Golf Club 1893 Presented by A. M. Ross". With the addition of a blue ribbon it became the Badge of Office and is still so used.

Another suggestion by the same retiring Captain was that the office of Vice-Captain be introduced. This was agreed.

In an effort to make the Club more attractive to active playing members five Medal Competitions were introduced in the summer of 1975. In September that year an Invitation Foursomes Competition was held for the first time and for it a Silver Quaich was presented as trophy by Mrs Chalmers in memory of her late husband Mr W. M. Chalmers, a former member. Further competitions were introduced over the years and a Club Championship inaugurated in 1980.

In 1979 a Club Tie was adopted and a new Club Flag designed. A "200" Club was formed as a fund-raising measure, but the highlight of that year was the purchase of the links. At a Special General Meeting held on 26 May 1979 members approved the purchase of the course and unfettered ownership of the Clubhouse and its surrounds, all at a cost of £150,000. The area involved was approximately 212 acres. Finance was raised by the compulsory levy of Membership Deposits repayable without interest on death or resignation, and the issue of Unsecured Loan Stock which carried no interest but gave a rebate on the annual subscription.

By September 1979 moneys raised for the purchase of the course totalled £154,892 made up as follows:

554 Membership Deposits	£61,515
87 Cash gifts	5,777
226 Loan Stock Applications	87,600
	£154,892

114 members declared their Deposits, totalling £12,730, as non-returnable, i.e., a gift. In subsequent years many members showed further considerable generosity by gifting Deposits and Loan Stock. In 1982 Membership Deposits were no longer required from new members but Entrance Fees were increased substantially.

The Club was incorporated as a Limited Company (Limited by Guarantee) on 20 June 1979 and started trading on 11 November 1979 by taking over the assets and liabilities of Luffness New Golf Club. To celebrate the purchase of the course a new competition was inaugurated, The Foundation Foursomes, and first held in July 1979. Father and son members, W. D. and M. D. Mayer, presented a trophy for this competition, known as The Mayer Goblet. In the summer of 1983 a cocktail party was held for the first time. This became an annual event held on the evening of the Foundation Foursomes.

In 1983 that part of the course lying to the west of the main road, holes 6-18, was designated a Site of Special Scientific Interest under the Wildlife and Countryside Act 1981. Fortunately this did not lead to any greenkeeping problems.

At intervals over the years suggestions have been made to protect the rough and many golfers will have their own story to tell of their ventures into the "tiger" country. A brief quote from the Agronomist's Report in 1979 states:

"Some criticisms of the rough have been made and these were investigated. The rough is of course characteristic of the links of Gullane Hill and mowing it would be sacrilege. Firstly, it would take years to recover and without the rough the entire character of the course would disappear and many of the holes on Luffness would be the poorer. Secondly, when or if the rough did recover, it would be far thicker in the bottom and therefore even worse a problem."

Finally in this decade, Mr James Falconer relinquished office as Secretary and Treasurer on 11 November 1983 and was succeeded by Mr Alex Hogg.

Tailpiece:

1974 — John Le Carre published *Tinker, Tailor, Soldier, Spy*.

1978 — The world's first test-tube baby was born at Oldham General Hospital.

1983 — The wearing of seat belts in the front seats of cars became compulsory.

1984-1993

By the mid-1980s the popularity of the game of golf had grown to such an extent that many clubs received an upsurge in applications for membership. This demand did not escape Luffness New.

The limit for Ordinary Membership was increased at the end of 1985 from 450 to 475, and by 1987 a large Waiting List had been built up. In June 1989 when there were 111 applicants awaiting entry, the Waiting List for Ordinary and Five-day Members was closed until further notice. Two years later there were still 100 on the list with 86 awaiting application forms when the list re-opened.

The 'eighties saw a revival in the national economy and for many this was a period of increasing affluence and leisure. The Club was in a very healthy state including financially. There was an active membership and an increasing number of members' guests and those playing with visiting societies enjoyed the excellent facilities of the Course and Clubhouse.

Mr Alex Hogg resigned as Secretary in May 1985 and was replaced by Mr R. S. Murray. He demitted office in 1986 and was succeeded by Lieutenant-Colonel Ian Tedford, the first Secretary of the Club to be a retired member of Her Majesty's Forces. Of the 13 Secretaries to date there have been three lawyers, five chartered accountants, one retired Scottish banker, one retired international banker, one retired police officer, one retired mining engineer and currently a retired army officer.

In October 1985 Mr Alan Guthrie intimated his resignation as Clubmaster, on medical grounds, and was succeeded by Mr G. Foreman. He resigned 18 months later and was replaced in July 1987 by Mr J. J. Little with Mrs Little in charge of the catering.

During the period 1987-92 a major programme of Club extensions and refurbishment, including the installation of gas central heating, was carried out. This added greatly to the Club amenities whilst preserving the dignified character and unique atmosphere of the Clubhouse. The greenkeepers' "bothy" was not forgotten and this was included in the refurbishment programme.

In April 1991 the installation of a watering system of pop-up sprinklers to the greens, tees and fairways was completed at a cost of £146,965.

The sporting highlight of this decade was the winning of the East Lothian County Cup in 1988 when the Club team consisted of Messrs

C. Cuthbert, T. M. Lamb, R. M. Gaunt and C. L. Wood. This was only the third time the Club had been successful in this tournament, the previous successes being in 1898 and 1951.

East Lothian County Cup Winners, 1988

C. Cuthbert and T. M. Lamb,   *R. M. Gaunt and C. L. Wood,*
First Couple   *Second Couple*

In 1986 the spartan-like drinking tap near the 9th green was replaced by a fountain erected in memory of David Lawrie, a loyal and popular member of the Club, who had been Champion in 1965, 1968 and 1976 of The Society of One Armed Golfers.

In 1987 a new Club Flag was introduced, green with a saltire cross in yellow, with the addition of the letters ''LNGC''. This replaced the 1979 flag which was also green and had the shield from the Club Tie together with the scroll ''Ceux des Luffness''. The shield and scroll were associated with the Arms of the Bickerton family who were granted the Barony of Luffness in the 14th century by David II. Prior to 1979 the Club Flag was similar to a Red Ensign with the letters ''LNGC'' boldly displayed on white on the red portion of the flag. The origin of this flag is not recorded.

An alternative Club Tie was brought into use in 1987. This was striped and thought to be more appropriate than the original tie for wear with a suit. Three years later bow ties were introduced in the colours of the alternative tie.

In 1992 the course was once again one of the venues for the Final Qualifying Competition for the Open Championship as it had been since 1966 whenever the Championship was played at Muirfield.

In the story of Luffness New we have noted the adverse effect on the course of the lack of rain. However, the climate is generally mild and the tiny strip of land north of a line drawn approximately from Longniddry Railway Station to the Bass Rock, benefits from one of the last surges of a branch of the Gulf Stream as it edges into the Firth of Forth. The Luffness climate is not unlike that of the Moray Firth which also benefits from the Gulf Stream. It is a frequent occurrence for members to telephone the Club from Edinburgh where the weather might be atrocious, and to be told that conditions at Luffness are more benign and the course playable.

Over the years many members and friends have made generous gifts to the Club of legacies, valuable paintings and golfing memorabilia, etc. These are too numerous to mention in this short history but the generosity is greatly appreciated and has been duly recorded in the Club records.

Luffness Mill Course — 1894   *Luffness New Course — 1994*

See maps on inside front and back covers

	Name	Yards		Name	Yards
1.	Mill	330	1.	Luffness Mill	332
2.	Saltcoats	215	2.	Saltcoats	420
3.	Castle	250	3.	Gullane	196
4.	Long — Out	450	4.	Long	531
5.	Quarry	336	5.	Milestone	326
6.	Hill	330	6.	Quarry	155
7.	Short — Out	160	7.	Hill	293
8.	March	270	8.	March	383
9.	Inchkeith	330	9.	Inchkeith	427
10.	Short — In	170	10.	Benty	176
11.	Fenton Tower	286	11.	Peffer Bank	445
12.	North Berwick Law	290	12.	Luffness	336
13.	Road	280	13.	Well	393
14.	Teapot	320	14.	Aberlady	435
15.	Aberlady	430	15.	Road	346
16.	Luffness	176	16.	Warren	163
17.	Plantation	250	17.	Plantation	349
18.	Home	462	18.	Home	416
		5,335			6,122

LUFFNESS HOUSE

HENRY WALTER HOPE

by

GEORGE HOPE

Henry Walter Hope was born in 1839, the third child and second son of George William Hope and his wife Caroline. He died in 1913, having inherited Luffness in 1863, when his father died at the comparatively early age of fifty-five. He had six brothers and two sisters, but most of them never married, and in the next generation there were only four children, two boys and two girls. Of these, one was Henry's only child, George Everard Hope.

Henry's paternal grandfather was Sir Alexander Hope, a younger son of the 2nd Earl of Hopetoun, born when his father was aged sixty-five. Nor was Sir Alexander the youngest in the family. He had three younger sisters, one of whom married her cousin, Lord President Hope, and was the ancestress of the current Lord President of the Court of Session.

Both Sir Alexander and George William were Members of Parliament, so they and their families were much in the south. Sir Alexander sent his sons to Harrow, but George William, doubtless only too acutely aware of what a mistake that was, sent his sons to Eton. James Hope-Scott, George William's younger brother, went one better. He had strong views on education and was one of the founders of Glenalmond. Unfortunately, he blotted his copybook irredeemably by becoming a Papist and, as a result, all reference to him was expunged even to the extent of cutting him out of the prayers. Few in the school now know of him.

Henry, on leaving Eton, went into the Grenadier Guards, his grandfather's old regiment. In those days, Household troops did not

37

serve out of the country except in time of war. It is interesting to note that a Guards Brigade, including the 2nd Battalion Grenadiers, in which Henry was serving, was posted to Canada in the early 1860s. There had been an incident involving two ships, and it was an open secret, since often denied, that Great Britain was preparing to enter the American Civil War on the side of the South.

Unfortunately the anti-slavery lobby was able to scupper this admirable scheme, and Great Britain stayed neutral. It is clear, however, from the photograph albums at Luffness, that serving officers were happily going on jaunts into the United States. Was it reconnaissance? We shall never know.

On the death of his father, Henry came out of the army, but, judging by the entries in the Family Bible, it took him some time to get home. His elder brother, Alexander, had died young, so at the age of 24, Henry found himself proprietor not only of Luffness, but also of Rankeillour, in Fife. On arrival back in Scotland it was not long before he, together with Lord Wemyss, founded Luffness Golf Club. Also, at Rankeillour, Henry discovered that one of his under-gardeners, one Tom Morris, not only shared his love of the game, but was a remarkably good player. He encouraged young Mr Morris and helped him embark on his career as a professional; they remained good friends until Henry's death.

Meanwhile, the feud between Luffness and Gosford that was to dominate the Parish of Aberlady for decades, began. It looks as if it all may well have started over pheasants, so, not to be partisan, here is a Gosford story about one aspect of the quarrel.

The Gosford Kennels, where much pheasant rearing took place, lie only about a hundred yards from the Luffness march. Apparently, the Luffness keeper, during the weeks before a shoot, used to sow the area just over the march with delicacies like raisins, thus persuading the Gosford birds that the Luffness side of the march was the place to feed. On the morning of the shoot the beaters, watched by the helpless Gosford keeper, lined up along the march and, shouting jubilantly, drove the birds eastward to Maggie's Wa's and the guns.

Of course, keepers are never as helpless as they like to make out, and, the dates of shoots being public knowledge, such behaviour would only have worked once. Whatever else may have been true, warfare existed on the march and it was not long before the two proprietors found themselves manoeuvred, willingly or otherwise, into public support of their staff. Over the years, the people of Aberlady found themselves unable to avoid taking sides, and it was not until after the last war that the mutual antagonisms began to be at last dismantled.

Looking back now, the feud appears funny rather than serious, and the moves of the various participants seem to be those of comic opera rather than of real life. Some fishing boats were wrecked in Gosford

38

Bay and Lord Wemyss considered the wrecks romantic.·Henry bribed a tramp to set them on fire. In the fullness of time another set of wrecks appeared, this time in Aberlady Bay, which Henry, in turn, liked the look of. Lord Wemyss was more subtle, however. He used his position on the County Council to nobble the Sanitary Officer, who had them removed at public expense, as a danger to public health.

Both men served on the County Council, and it used to be said that before any meeting started Lord Wemyss would look round and with great good nature say "Mornin', Henry", to which the reply would come "My name's Hope". This formality over, the business of the day proceeded.

As far as golf is concerned, the feud led to the end of the old Luffness Golf Club, and the laying out of two new courses, Luffness New Golf Club and Kilspindie. Kilspindie likes to contend that it is the old club continuing, and maintains that it has irrefutable documentary evidence to back up the claim. Be that as it may, there was certainly a clean break when the old club came to an end. Such a claim, though, was just the sort of thing calculated to annoy Henry, and is as likely to have been carefully contrived as to have been true. No chance was missed of keeping animosity alive, and the two clubs took their places with enthusiasm on opposite sides in the fight.

Luffness New Golf Club was laid out by Henry and Tom Morris, very much as a joint effort. In the first two decades of its existence the initial design, which incorporated, almost unaltered, some of the fairways of the old course, was changed extensively. One can only guess that this was, in part, because of changing demand, generated by changes in the game and the club membership.

All this must be seen in the context of the building boom with the considerable changes in topography at that time in the whole area. The Aberlady and Gullane Railway Line was built after extensive lobbying behind the scenes from members of the Honourable Company of Edinburgh Golfers. who wished to make their new course at Muirfield more accessible. Henry himself built the Marine Hotel, Gullane (now the Fire Training School) at the end of that line, largely to cater to the visiting golfer. His crest, and the date of construction, can still be seen over the door. On a different scale, Henry's sister Lucy built the Hope Rooms in North Berwick. There must have been enormous pressures on the locality, all now for practical purposes forgotten, which are in some ways not unlike those currently being exerted.

Apart from golf, Henry was a keen shot, and also rode to hounds. In those days both sports were governed, in a way that nowadays is hard to appreciate, by the limitations of horse transport. True, there were railways, but as often as not a day's shooting or hunting meant rising well before dawn and hacking for miles, in order to arrive in time. A book on Whittinghame published not so long ago shows that

Henry was prepared to travel that far for a shoot. As far as hunting is concerned, the East Lothian Hounds' last Meet was in the mid-1890s, near Dunbar, Henry being their last Master. In those days, most of the rest of the county was fox-free. Would that were still the case!

Henry was well connected as well as having achievements of his own that speak for themselves. Among other distinctions he was Provincial Grand Master of the Masons. Lord Leconfield, the first Captain of Luffness New Golf Club, was his wife's brother-in-law. His wife was Lady Mary Primrose, sister of Lord Rosebery, next Liberal Prime Minister after Gladstone.

Although never a Liberal, it was at that time that Henry made his unsuccessful attempt to start an agricultural workers' union. Doubtless trades unions were looked on with favour in some Liberal circles, but the thought of Lord Wemyss waking up to find large numbers of his estate workers signed up in Henry's union is one that must have been sweet.

If two things shine through all accounts of Henry's life, they are first his invariable kindness, and second the great loyalty of which he was capable, particularly when it was to someone less well placed than himself. This was in full measure repaid, for he was also the recipient of great loyalty. He was an eccentric, which meant that he was always unpredictable, but he was never unfair or unjust.

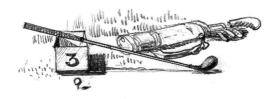

In 1940 a "Luffness" Kummel cost 2/6, while Cherry Brandy was 2/-.

Recipe for a Golfer's sponge—3 "Fores"
   4 Yolks of eggs
   4 Tablespoons of flour
   4 Tablespoons of sugar.

AT SOME HOLES RABBITS ARE VERY ACTIVE

THE COURSE

by

HAMISH STEVEN

The Luffness members, despite the camaraderie and friendship within the Clubhouse, have always insisted that the main criterion for membership is for the pursuance of the game of golf. To this end, they have made sure that the state of the course has priority. Fortunately, over the generations, they have been supported and indeed led by the Greenkeeping staff who have never been afraid to take on mammoth tasks if the necessity arose. A few years ago, the Head Greenkeeper, Bob Watt, despite a heavy load of winter work, insisted that his staff wanted to place an additional bunker on the right of the fourth fairway to tighten up the hole. Too many members were playing wide on the right, and receiving no punishment. ''Ah'm havin' naebody makin' a bloody fool out o' ma course,'' he said, ''even if it means a bit o' extra work fur me an' the lads.'' This is the attitude of staff which makes this Club and course the place of enjoyment it is for members and, we hope, their guests.

The course is not long in yards and it is always possible to score well in favourable conditions. However, such conditions are rare on most seaside courses and Luffness is no exception. The wind can be very demanding and the first two and last two holes, into an east wind, have ruined many a scorecard. The yardage on the course can be reduced considerably by use of front ''visitors'' tees which can give a misleading view of the problems. It is interesting to note the variety of tees in approximately the same location but at different sides of the fairway giving a totally different angle to the hole.

1st Hole: "Luffness Mill" 332 yards par 4. The second shot at this hole is considered by many to be the hardest shot on the course. This could be a reflection on one's partner's drive in this stronghold of foursome golf, or simply the result of a good lunch.

2nd Hole: "Saltcoats" 420 yards par 4. This hole is at its most difficult into an east wind when it is probably best treated as a 5. Never an easy hole but all the problems are there to be seen.

3rd Hole: "Gullane" 196 yards par 3. Into a strong breeze, this is one of the best short holes in golf. When the ground is dry members never give a putt. Borrows can be extremely hard to read, and a putt from the top edge, running off the green at the bottom, is not unknown.

4th Hole: "Long" 531 yards par 5. This, the longest hole on the course is the only one that never plays below its par, even in favourable conditions. It has often been suggested that this would make an excellent last hole as the green is in sight of the Clubhouse.

5th Hole: "Milestone" 326 yards par 4. Apparently straightforward, but as it is usually played with a strong crosswind, the severe rough on either side has magnetic attraction for the careless. The senior members probably have greatest success at this hole with two full woods to the heart of the green followed by a putt for a birdie.

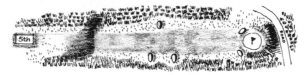

6th Hole: "Quarry" 155 yards par 3. Although ringed with bunkers, this short hole has no secrets. The tee, however, is sheltered, and one forgets the wind. Stories of the original difficulties of this hole when the drive was over the quarry will be found elsewhere.

7th Hole: "Hill" 293 yards par 4. This blind drive uphill is appropriately assisted by the white painted stone behind the flag, which is certainly a good line for a long drive. For the average golfer, however, the difficulty lies in judging the second shot. As the green is long and thin, careful assessment of the pin position is paramount. Many petitions have been submitted that this hole as stroke one is nonsense, the claim being that this cannot conform with any known golf regulation. The consistent answer to this query is typical of the approach of Luffness members to the game—"it's like that because the senior members need a shot up that hill".

8th Hole: "March" 383 yards par 4. The name here describes this hole's position bordering the Club's neighbours and friendly rivals at Gullane Golf Club. The tee high on Gullane Hill gives one of the most spectacular scenes in the district. The more experienced player on this hole, however, keeps his head down on this tee shot, as any drive not struck properly can drift a long way in the wind. Strangely, one has never heard of Luffness members being asked for a green fee for Gullane No. 3, although the reverse has often been suggested. This is perhaps the only hole where luck frequently plays too big a part;

the lie of the land and the slope running off the green makes the approach shots more a flirtation with lady luck than a question of skill.

9th Hole: "Inchkeith" 427 yards par 4. Many an outward half has been ruined by this hole especially into a west wind in the winter when the ground is very dead at the front of the green. Truly, it sometimes feels as if one has hit enough shots to reach the isle of Inchkeith which appears just off the sandbanks.

10th Hole: "Benty" 176 yards par 3. This innocuous looking short hole produces a par far too infrequently. A quantity of sand was blown onto the fairway from the beach in 1983 as a result of which, any ball hit short of the green tends to stop very quickly.

11th Hole: "Peffer Bank" 445 yards par 4. If a shot is dropped at the 9th hole into the predominant west wind, this hole will play shorter and the medal player has the opportunity to recover here. The hole is very similar to the 9th for in summer both aprons become very fiery and mishit seconds will be punished wherever they finish off the green.

12th Hole: "Luffness" 336 yards par 4. Like many links courses Luffness has its loop which can make or mar any card. The 12/13/14/15 are all par 4. At least one of these will play as a 5 depending once again on that fickle lady the wind. This loop is a favourite place for eider ducks to nest. These feathery friends, in addition to being one of the features of Luffness golf, help to exemplify the gentlemanly sportsmanship of this bastion of all male foursome golf. Where else would you see the rules of golf being set aside to allow four golfers to discuss whether to allow a free "lift and drop" in the rough, in order to avoid disturbing an eider hen sitting on her nest?

13th Hole: "Well" 393 yards par 4. The origin of the name of this hole is not known but it could easily be a reiteration of the most common exclamation by members having completed the hole. The prevailing head on left to right wind makes this green difficult to hit in two, and any straying off the fairway is harshly punished.

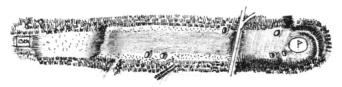

14th Hole: "Aberlady" 435 yards par 4. The name expresses well the feeling of a senior member having hit three good woods and still finding himself short of all the bunkers in front of the green. This hole, rated highly as a par 4 by many top golfers, has in place a championship tee behind the 13th green making the hole some 50 yards longer. Despite perhaps a justifiable criticism that the course could do with additional yardage, it is generally agreed that in this instance it would turn a good four into a poor five.

15th Hole: "Road" 346 yards par 4. With the prevailing wind now "up the kilt" on the way home, this is the start of a chance to pick up shots. While all seems straightforward, in the heat of the moment it is too easy to forget the angle of the bunkers guarding this green, carefully placed by Mr Henry Walter Hope and Mr Tom Morris, the architects of this fine course. As a result one too often drops into one of these traps or otherwise misjudges line and length. The road which gives the hole its name can barely be seen today, crossing the fairway on the length of a good drive.

16th Hole: "Warren" 163 yards par 3. This straightforward hole with a green ringed with bunkers presents one major problem on the tee. The correct choice of club is imperative. It can vary from a 2 iron to a wedge. There would seem to be a tendency to underclub for one rarely sees a player entangled in the buckthorn behind the green which is the home of many rabbits. Any player looking back here at a card with four par 3s at the short holes will surely be heading for a happy lunch.

17th Hole: "Plantation" 349 yards par 4. The tee can be of great importance here as well as the ever present wind. Into a cold east wind the last two holes can (and do) turn a player to drink. In normal conditions the hole should be played down the left. Punishing bunkers on the right await a misdirected drive and experience dictates that a pitch in from the left is more likely to give a player a putt for a three. This assumes that one remembers the hollow on the right edge of the green which has ruined many a card and decided many a match. The row of bunkers 20 yards in front of the green should not come into play with modern golf equipment except, perhaps, for a "carelessly" long hit drive.

46

18th Hole: "Home" 416 yards par 4. A fine last hole by any standards. Always difficult to hit the green in two and even more difficult to get down in two more for your par 4 if you don't. Study of experts at successive "Open" qualifying rounds would indicate that it is imperative to be up to the pin with the second shot, but then players of that class can play the chip off the dreaded bank.

Enjoy your round and the chat after.

"Never concede a short putt. For all the time that it takes—see it in."—Bill Chapman.

"Of course, golf is a left-handed game."—Stewart Stephen.

Your ball is five feet from the hole and you have two shots for a win—a voice says: "We'll see the first one."—Ian McGregor.

LUFFNESS NEW GOLF CLUB
CAPTAINS

Lord Leconfield	1894-1895
Lord Trayner	1895-1896
Major David Kinloch	1896-1897
A. Mackenzie Ross	1897-1898
W. G. Bloxsom	1898-1899
W. T. Armour	1899-1901
Rev. John Kerr	1901-1902
David Lyell	1902-1904
H. D. Lawrie	1904-1906
A. W. Robertson Durham	1906-1908
George E. Hope	1908-1911
Ian Macintyre	1911-1914
J. A. Robertson Durham	1914-1920
William Greenhill	1920-1922
William Robertson	1922-1925
P. J. Pringle	1925-1926
Fred Marshall	1926-1928
M. Cecil Butcher	1928-1930
T. Drybrough	1930-1932
A. D. F. Torrance	1932-1933
W. B. Torrance	1933-1935
A. Spottiswoode Ritchie	1935-1937
Dr A. Cleland	1937-1946
James M. Cooper	1946-1948
Stanley Ramsden	1948-1950
John S. Wells	1950-1952
John L. Sommerville	1952-1953
Sir John L. Sommerville	1953-1954
A. A. Innes Wedderburn	1954-1956
R. Leslie Stewart	1956-1958
Stanley Bennet	1958-1960

R. Ian Marshall	1960-1962
James J. Carmichael	1962-1964
C. G. Wallace	1964-1966
T. C. Scott	1966-1968
John Graham	1968-1970
J. D. W. Spence	1970-1972
Dr W. Donald MacLennan	1972-1974
Alex Mason	1974-1976
R. W. Gardiner	1976-1978
Dr D. R. Sandison	1978-1980
H. S. U. Steven	1980-1982
W. D. Henderson	1982-1984
G. A. Henry	1984-1986
J. H. Marshall	1986-1989
Dr G. Kennedy	1989-1991
J. A. M. Snow	1991-1993
N. B. Richardson	1993-19

CLUB CAPTAINS—PAST AND PRESENT

Back row, left to right: Jim Snow, Douglas Henderson, Hamish Steven, Gilbert Kennedy, John Marshall, George Henry.
Front row, left to right: Donald Sandison, Tom Scott, Nigel Richardson (present Captain), "Buster" Wallace, Bill MacLennan.

RUFFNESS?

AN AGRONOMIST OBSERVES
by

J. H. ARTHUR, B.Sc.(Agric.)

Luffness New has always been one of my favourite links—and indeed favourite clubs, which is not necessarily always the same thing. My appreciation goes back well over forty years, in which time so many of our links courses have lost the one characteristic that puts them so far above all others, namely the dominance of links grasses and above all their fine fescue turf.

What has achieved this miracle? Without a doubt it is continuity of correct and traditional management. The use of a greens committee was practised briefly and with a degree of limited enthusiasm prior to the Second World War, but the opinion of the Head Greenkeeper has always been respected and still is today. The very small number of Head Greenkeepers employed at Luffness New over the past century is testimony to the confidence in their ability. James King, whose service spanned a period of some thirty-three years, tersely observed "You can please yourself, Gentlemen, but there will be **no** greens committee on my course". There still is not one. And that above all else has guaranteed the continuity of correct management, and the avoidance of costly mistakes, which has ensured that fine fescues dominate the entire links and notably those superb greens. We hear so much of the need for speed of putting surface, which has resulted in all manner of ignominious treatments being meted out to long suffering greens—and especially shaving to ridiculously low heights for long periods. This kills the grass, or at least permits meadow grass dominance. Luffness greens are as fast as anyone could reasonably require, because they are fescue greens, and they are as good in winter as in late spring.

Luffness management has always had the sense to listen to their head men. In Bob Watt you have today not only a dedicated and skilled head man, staunchly defending time proven traditional methods, but in addition a worthy successor to the small number of Head Greenkeepers employed to date. Luffness owes them a great deal.

What then is this traditional management? It can easily be summed up in the continued responsible delegation of course supervision to those who know best. Furthermore it costs less, both to implement and also because it creates far less management problems, compared with maintaining turf artificially, when it is naturally so much more susceptible to poor drought, resistance to pest, and reduced wear resistance.

The principle behind the entire policy is to listen to what the grass has to tell you. Our links grasses which made the game of golf possible (which came first?) have not altered since time began, and have taken half a million years to become adapted to thin, sandy, poverty striken soils. Were our links (and indeed moorland and heathlands) not so inherently infertile and so difficult to "improve"

GREENKEEPING STAFF

Left to right: John Mercer, Robert Watt Jnr., Jim Notman, Alan Burnett, David Coull, "Bob" Watt (Head Greenkeeper), Fraser Hirst.

in agricultural terms, they would centuries ago have been taken into cultivation. In fact it was a renowned Professor of Geology who commented that Europe's scenery owes much to toxicity—soils so poor or so acid that they could never be cropped economically.

The needs of these links grasses have never altered. They can happily thrive in conditions of minimal soil nutrient status. Why then should we try to give them what they do not want?

The simple fact that golf is played on links turf does not create manurial deficiencies, but it does create compaction, and this can be counteracted by aeration. In the old days this was often done—and indeed I have seen it done at Luffness New by a line of greenkeepers inserting graips at close spacing, levering back, and then moving back a few inches to start the process all over again. This in fact is the same principle on which the Vertidrain works—a machine going deeper and using less men, but the same idea, nearly a century later.

In the early days, Luffness greens were dressed with soot and sand—and soot is a nitrogenous fertiliser. Today we still use the same mixture as fifty years ago, a mix of organic and inorganic nitrogen sparingly applied perhaps twice a year. Not for us "modern" man made fertilisers, nor do we want, and therefore we do not use, phosphates, which permit the invasion of more fertility loving grasses.

As for top dressing—to achieve true putting surfaces, this has always been based on improving the humus (water and nutrient retaining) content of the local black sandy soil. Today we use machines to prepare and spread it—where once it was sheer man-power.

Nothing changes, because the needs of the grasses have not changed. *Plus ca change, plus c'est la même chose!* Only today we have to do the same thing more quickly to minimise interference with play and to counteract its consolidating effect on sandy soil which otherwise would inhibit deep rooting links grasses, and encourage the shallow rooting ones which have so ruined many of our famous links.

The saving grace of Luffness New has been that for so many years there was no money with which to make mistakes, combined with inspired understanding that our links grasses do not want pampering—and need not be green! A shower or two of rain after the summer drought has left the course a pale shade of khaki—and hey presto, everything greens over, and the links grasses survive where the undesirable ones are thinned out.

This is the reasoning behind the remark in one of my last reports to the Club—"If all my advisory visits were like those at Luffness New, my work would be a sinecure. It does me good to see how good course conditions can be when other clubs with severe problems blame the weather or the amount of play." I should have added that all my visits would have been visits of unalloyed pleasure.

No words of mine can describe a late autumn visit to Luffness, with its springy fine turf and the evening sky filled with skeins of geese flighting in to Aberlady Bay, contrasting so much with the early summer sights of wildflower strewn rough, not to mention the rabbits, whose depredations onto sacrosanct turf areas caused us all so many sleepless nights in the run up to the Open Championships.

Yes, Luffness is high on the list of my most favourite clubs, unspoilt but not unspoilable, blessed equally by superb surroundings and devoted staff, a wonderful test of golf and an excellent example of what true links golf is all about. To cap that may be impossible, but few clubs of all the hundreds I used to visit in over forty years of advisory work, have been more warmly welcoming and genuinely friendly.

Here's to the next hundred years.

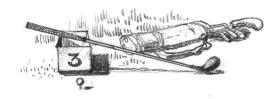

Just after the introduction of decimalisation an elderly Member rang for the Steward. "I'd like two markers please," whereupon these were placed on the counter. "How much are they?" asked the venerable gentleman. "A penny each," was the reply. The old man produced a sixpenny piece and was given a halfpenny in his change. "Och, I hate these coins," he said. "They're no use to anyone." "With respect, Sir," said the Steward, "They're excellent as ball markers and at only half the price."—Ian Melrose.

FREDDIE TAIT

by

ROBIN WELSH

Freddie Tait, one of the first life members when Luffness New Golf Club was founded in 1894, is the "father figure" of the Club. Three photographs of him hang on the walls. His putter lies in a showcase above the bar. Echoes of his personality still pervade the clubroom.

Frederick Guthrie Tait was born in Edinburgh on 11 January 1870. His father, Professor of Natural Philosophy at Edinburgh University, spent much of his free time on the links at St Andrews and was also interested in the mechanics of the game.

When Freddie grew to full stature, he helped his father in experiments to ascertain the initial velocity of a well-driven ball and wrote in 1896: "We think we have at last arrived at the truth (220 feet per second)."

Reared in such a sporting atmosphere, it was natural that Freddie would be introduced to golf at an early age. A photograph of him as a sailor-suited slip of a lad swinging a club confirms the fact—and there is the remarkable story of Lieutenant Tait of the Black Watch who, when serving as a member of Her Majesty's Guard at Balmoral, met Queen Victoria and was introduced to the Tsar of Russia.

The Tsar asked him when he had started to play golf. Freddie replied: "I took to it seriously when I was eight years old!"

Freddie Tait entered Edinburgh Academy in 1881. A year later, at the age of 12, he played in an Under-15 Academy golf tournament on the Musselburgh Links and came second. It was his first golfing prize. Later in the year, he broke 100 for the first time.

He maintained his connection with Edinburgh Academy throughout his life. Before sailing on his ill-fated journey to South Africa in October 1899, his steamer was delayed by fog at Tilbury and he wired Edinburgh to ascertain the result of the Edinburgh Academicals' rugby match against Watsonians.

Freddie Tait was killed leading his Company in an attack on a Boer position of Koodoosberg Drift in February 1900. Shot in the chest, he died instantaneously. He was 30 years old.

In his short life, he achieved legendary status, not only through his fame as a golfer but also because of his qualities of sportsmanship and his open, enthusiastic nature. Contemporary sources all testify to the magnetism of his personality and his immense popularity.

This tribute deals chronologically with some of the principal events in Freddie Tait's life.

He left Edinburgh Academy in 1883 for Sedbergh where his house master wrote of him: "He is a thoroughly jolly boy with any amount of backbone developing itself." In his first year, he saved a school friend from drowning during a walk in the Yorkshire Fells. In his last year he gained his colours in the First Fifteen.

In 1888, he attended Edinburgh University for a year prior to entering Sandhurst where he explained the mysteries of golf to his fellow cadets. In 1890, he was gazetted to the Leinster Regiment.

The same year, he joined the Royal and Ancient Golf Club and played against and beat the brothers Blackwell, J. E. Laidlay, who won the Amateur Championship the following year, and other famous St Andrews names, including Andrew Kirkcaldy and Willie Auchterlonie.

In Edinburgh, for two months before joining his Regiment, he played rugby for Edinburgh Wanderers and Ian McIntyre, President of the Scottish Rugby Union and Captain of the Wanderers Club, wrote of him: "It is my deliberate opinion at that time, that Tait was one of the very best forwards playing in Edinburgh, if not in Scotland." Later, when based in Edinburgh Castle with the Black Watch, he played rugby for Edinburgh Academicals (1894-95).

Powerfully built, with an aptitude for sport, he played cricket for the Grange Club, was an excellent shot and was fond of curling—but, as he wrote to his brother Jack, "curling in the country is where you meet ploughmen and gardeners and get plenty of excitement, not in the Coates Club (Edinburgh) where you only meet judges, lawyers, businessmen and that sort of crowd!"

But golf was his consuming passion. In his teens and early twenties, he was noted principally for his prodigious driving. On his twenty-third birthday, 11 January 1893, he hit a drive at the 13th hole at St Andrews which became a celebrated talking point. On hard ground with no wind, the drive measured 341 yards, with a carry of 250 yards. Later, he harnessed his power and became a wonderfully consistent driver, long and straight.

Young Freddie Tait—aet 6 years.

Tait in action.

58

In 1894, prior to joining the 2nd Battalion, the Black Watch, he scored 72s at St Andrews and Carnoustie, both records, and, in 1895, became a founder member of Luffness New, winning the first medal with a 76 in his first game on the course.

The year, 1896, became known as "Tait's Year", mainly because of his performances in the St George's Vase and the Amateur Championship at Sandwich, both of which he won.

He gave notice of his form in March that year, going round Muirfield in 73. In the Open Championship on the same course, he finished third behind the great professionals Vardon and Taylor. He scored 74 on the newly-extended course at North Berwick and, a day later, beat Ben Sayers who said of his defeat: "Beaten by eight holes on my own green—it's no possible but it's a fac'!"

In the 1896 Amateur Championship, he beat a formidable group of the top players of the day in successive rounds—Charles Hutchings, J. E. Laidlay, John Ball, Horace Hutchinson and, in the final, Harold Hilton.

Of Tait's victory, Hilton wrote: "I never witnessed finer golf than that displayed by F. G. Tait. His driving, although probably not quite as long as of yore, was infinitely more accurate than we have been accustomed to associate with the champion. I had never yet seen more accurate play from the tee and through the green. He has always had the reputation of being a good putter and he certainly did not fail to act up to that reputation, his holing out at two or three yards being marvellously correct. In fact, it was golf of the finest order and the sensational part of the performance was almost lost in the machine-like accuracy with which the holes were played!"

The Amateur Cup was given pride of place with the other trophies which decorated the Black Watch mess table. Among the tributes received by Tait was honorary membership of the Royal Burgess Golfing Society.

Tait also won the Amateur Championship at Hoylake and the St George's Vase at Sandwich in 1898—and he renewed his connection with Luffness, leading the Club to victory in the East Lothian County Cup. He also played as often as he could in Luffness medals, the last occasion being in 1899 before he left for South Africa.

In 1899, he won the St George's Vase for the third time and was only just denied a hat trick of victories in the Amateur Championship when beaten by the famous Englishman, John Ball, at the 37th hole in the final.

Tait considered St Andrews, where he learned to play, as the best test of golf. Next in line he preferred Hoylake—"the finest of greens"—and, in his later years, the New Course at St Andrews and Luffness New were prime favourites.

Freddie Tait was the most charismatic golfer of his time. Crowds gathered wherever he played. Immensely strong, he hit the ball with controlled power and the stories of his recovery shots are legion. He was also a master of the pitch and run approach shot, perfected at St Andrews, and was recognised as one of the best putters in the game—with the old-fashioned cleek cut short which is now on display in the Luffness clubroom.

In addition, he was blessed with the ideal temperament for golf. Confident in his ability, philosophical about misfortune, he revelled in the fellowship and excitement of the game and, as a true amateur, enjoyed his golf.

Acknowledgements are made to the book, *F. G. Tait, A Record*, by John L. Low (1900) for most of the information in this tribute. John Low lost to Tait at the 22nd hole in the semi-final of the 1898 Amateur Championshnip at Hoylake.

In his book, Mr Low stressed the sporting nature of his subject. "He played the game as a Scottish gentleman, with dignity and strictness, tempered with unfailing courtesy."

In a letter to his brother in 1898, Tait wrote: "I can't say I care much for the score game." Mr Low underlined the point: "He preferred the cut and thrust of a match to medal play . . . and a congenial foursome gave him the greatest enjoyment of all."

How pleasant it is to know that, in this aspect at least, the modern Luffness members are following in the footsteps of the Club's "Father figure"!

In his day and in his own Scotland Freddie Tait was a national hero. I do not think I have ever seen any other golfer so adored by the crowd—no, not Harry Vardon nor Bobby Jones in their primes. It was a tremendous, and to his adversaries an almost terrifying popularity. He was only 30 when he was killed; a brave young man, like many others who were killed; a thoroughly friendly creature, who made friends with all sorts and conditions of men, but not in any way possessed of an outstanding mind and character.

He was just a thoroughly good fellow who played a game very skilfully.

Bernard Darwin.

THE GREENKEEPERS

HEAD GREENKEEPERS

1894- ?	G. Shepherd
1927-1929	J. Gault (possibly appointed pre-1927)
1929-1937	T. Martin
1937-1970	J. King
1970-1974	A. Thomson
1974-	R. Watt

THE END OF A PERFECT DAY.

CHARACTERS ALL

by

C. G. WALLACE

As could be expected in a Club where the competitive urge has always taken second place to the enjoyment of playing with one's friends, where foursome matchplay has mostly been preferred to singles, and where up until after World War II there were only two Medal Competitions each year, Luffness—apart from Freddie Tait—can claim but few really outstanding players. But characters we have always had. Can we meet some of them?

Lord Leconfield, first Captain 1894-95, was the brother-in-law of Henry W. Hope's wife, Lady Mary Primrose, sister of Lord Rosebery, Prime Minister 1894-95. He was 64 at the time he was appointed, and in April 1895 he presented our first Gold Medal for the best scratch score.

According to *Burke's Peerage*, he was a very substantial landowner in England and Ireland, being in 1883, twenty-fourth in order of acreage (some 66,000 in England between Cumberland, Sussex and Yorkshire; with 44,000 in Ireland, in Clare, Limerick and Tipperary), and tenth in order of income (£88,000). The Club clearly got off to a good start with a man of such substance at the helm. Apart from his family connections with the Hopes and Roseberys, he does not appear to have had any local interests in Scotland.

Our next Captain was **Lord Trayner**, a Law Lord. Having been an Advocate from 1858 and Sheriff of Forfar from 1881-85, he was appointed Judge in 1885. From 1889-98 he was a Railway Commissioner for Scotland (*ex officio*). Could he have leant his weight into the formation of the Gullane Branch line and the construction of the Luffness Halt?

He presided over an Extraordinary General Meeting on 28th February 1896 to raise the final £400 to complete the new Clubhouse to be ready for opening at the Spring Meeting in April, and he also presented the Trayner Cup, first played for in July that year. The original format was that of a knock-out competition, on handicap, over nine holes, played on the one day and with a restricted entry of thirty-two. The Luffness members dined Freddie Tait earlier that month at the Central Hotel (Edinburgh) in honour of his winning the Amateur Championship, and it is a reasonable assumption that Lord Trayner would have presided.

Rev. John Kerr, Captain 1901-02, was a very well-known figure, not only in East Lothian, but much further afield. He was born near Dumfries in 1853, graduated M.A. at Edinburgh, and was licensed as a minister by the Presbytery of Edinburgh in 1875. He had a charge at Skelmorlie briefly, before moving to Dirleton in 1878 where he remained until just before the Great War. He married in 1883 and is described as physically robust and vigorous. He expressed his views with great frankness, which possibly earned him some black marks in certain quarters. For instance, in 1901, he defended the Honourable Company of Edinburgh Golfers in their playing of Sunday golf, as they did not employ caddies or Club staff on the Sabbath, and several attended his service before going to play. He was progressive and active and popular with the locals to whom he was known as "Ready Money John".

His sporting activities were divided between golf and curling where he moved in the highest circles, being Chaplain to the Royal Caledonian Curling Club from 1897. He was very much *persona grata* amongst the East Lothian golfing gentry. He did, in fact, act as a golf reporter for two golfing periodicals, one of them *Golf*, later titled *Golf Illustrated*, under the pen name of "The Cornel".

He produced two very long and detailed works, *The Golf Book of East Lothian*, published in 1896, and an account of the R.C.C.C.'s trip to Canada and the U.S. in 1902-03. This latter is a massive and detailed tome of 788 pages, published in 1904, compiled from his experiences on the visit. The "East Lothian Golf Book" is to a large extent made up from his various reportings and is likewise a large volume with many illustrations now of considerable historical interest.

He was an original subscriber to Luffness New Golf Club. It is recorded that Freddie Tait in 1897 played him giving a stroke a hole and won by two holes, going round in 77. From this fact, the recorder of it deduced a handicap for John Kerr of 18. Whatever he achieved in office, one can be sure that the members' enjoyment of the course and Club would be enhanced by his strong character. He died in 1920 in Harrogate.

A. L. Glasgow (Alex) was connected with Luffness Golf Club for

38 years. Alex was officially appointed Clubmaster to the Luffness New Golf Club in 1912 and remained in office until his death in 1938 at the age of 63. He was married and had one son and two daughters, but his wife did not do the cooking and so he relied upon others for this service. "Bunty" Thomson provided a very high standard of

Alex Glasgow—Clubmaster, Luffness New G.C., 1912-1938.

cooking for many years, until she was "called up" in 1938 for War Service. In these days there were no Club Dinners but the Annual Dinner of the Club was an important item on the calendar when up to seven courses were served in the Clubhouse.

Alex was indeed a character, loved and respected by all. He had many friends embracing all social strata, including many famous golfers. He was generous. The story is told of the caddie who had been underpaid and requested support from Alex. His response was to dip into his own pocket to top up the caddie's inadequate fee. Ever popular, he was never more happy than when in the company of youngsters to whom he would jocularly comment, "Gi'e me a kiss, and lend me a bob"—undoubtedly our longest serving and a most prestigious Clubmaster.

Willie Torrance, W. B. as he was usually known to distinguish him from his brothers **A. D. F. (Fletcher)** and **T. A. (Tony)**, was one of the Club's most notable members in the inter-war years. In addition to Luffness, he was a member of the R. & A., Royal Burgess, Mortonhall and Gullane, but yet found time to win most of our trophies several times. His first success was the Hope Medal in 1920 which he won seven more times between then and 1938. He also won the Leconfield Gold Medal four times between 1922 and 1939. Our handicap trophies also bear his name over the same period.

The foregoing is all pretty parochial stuff, for not only did he play for Scotland in what are now called the Home Internationals from 1922-30, but he also played for Great Britain v. America in 1922, the first year when the Walker Cup was the prize. This was played at Long Island, New York, and, as was the pattern in these days, Great Britain lost 4-8. It would be pleasing if he had recorded even one win, but the sad fact is that he lost both foursome and singles matches. Competition was mighty tough in those days in that contest, and even his illustrious brother Tony, who played in five Walker Cup series, could only claim three wins and one halved match, one victim being the famous Francis Ouimet who went down 7 and 6. T. A. had no connection with Luffness being based in the south and playing most of his golf there.

W. B. took part in many outside amateur contests and won the St George's Cup at Sandwich in 1921, followed in 1931 by winning the Gleneagles Silver Tassie. He tied for first British amateur place in the Open of 1927. His name also appears on most of the trophies of the R. & A.

Despite all these widespread successes, he still found time to be a regular and devoted member of Luffness. His brother, A. D. F., was elected Captain in 1933 but sadly, he died very suddenly in his first year of office, and W. B. succeeded him in 1934 and went on to do a normal term of office, and thereafter was on the Committee. After the Second World War, he was a very regular weekend golfer, when his genial breezy presence was very much appreciated by his fellow members. In the usual Luffness tradition, he would get involved in many "bounce" games, regardless of the level of skill of the other participants. He was still a very formidable player and very competitive—a much sought after partner! If his long handicap partner duffed a shot, W. B.'s lower lip would project still further forward as he concentrated on the customary miraculous recovery shot, followed by a wide smile of satisfaction. Like his brother A. D. F., premature sudden death carried him off and Luffness lost a gentleman of immense character.

A **Caddiemaster**, who will remain anonymous, is referred to in the Minute of a Committee Meeting held on a Sunday (*Meetings* on

Sundays as well as *golf*), 25 September 1932. It reported that the Caddiemaster had been sentenced to forty days in prison for an offence under the National Insurance Acts. (The heinous crime of failing to disclose his immoral earnings as a caddie while drawing his dole money!) An impassioned plea from his wife for his reinstatement on release was submitted, and the Committee unanimously agreed to grant this. His contribution to the Club's well-being was obviously appreciated! He was a damned good caddie!

In August 1937, **James King**, an assistant greenkeeper at Gullane, was appointed Head Greenkeeper and commenced his long and very successful association with Luffness. He started with a weekly wage of £3 10/-, plus free house, coal and light, and was with us until he retired in 1970. Throughout all that time he kept the course in excellent condition, even through the problems and shortages of the war years. He was, in fact, in full-time service with the Royal Observer Corps from an early date in the war, and supervised the course in his spare time, an effort which caused him a duodenal ulcer from which he made a rapid and complete recovery. In the early sixties, he was approached unofficially by the R. & A. to see if he would be interested in becoming Links Supervisor there, but he preferred to stay with us in a job where he knew he was right on top.

Some few years before this, Bobby Locke, that celebrated South African player, had been playing on Luffness and was so much impressed with the greens that he stated they were the best he had ever played on and that he was prepared to give James King a written testimonial to that effect. King, in his usual modest manner, declined to put Bobby Locke to the trouble of writing such a document, stating "it wasnae necessary as a'body kens!". In 1973 when the course was suffering from the effects of prolonged drought, the Captain at that time visited him in his retirement to see if he could offer any help. His reply again was typical: "Dinnae worry, son—when the Good Lord decides to bring on the rain, it will sort itsel' out." He really was a sterling character and if further proof of his professional ability was required it came in the form of being awarded joint second place in the "Greenkeeper of the Year" award in 1969. When he retired, Luffness's loss was Aberlady Bowling Club's gain as he soon had it the envy of all the local greens.

Robin Wight won the Scottish Amateur at Muirfield in 1949 while he was a keen and active member of Luffness, but not surprisingly he entered from his local course, Glencorse, which marched with his farm at Oatslie. As far as Luffness is concerned his greatest achievement was being in the winning County Cup side in 1951 along with Jack Ness, Tom Scott and Alex Small, the Club's second success since 1898.

Robin tied for the Hope (Autumn) Medal in 1952 and won the Trayner Cup (Summer) in 1954. Partnered by H. J. Porteous, they were a formidable pair in the Winter Foursomes. Although they won it only once in 1956/57, they were runners-up and semi-finalists many times in the 'fifties and 'sixties. Robin, like all golfers of real class, had the ability to raise his game when the chips were down. If he was a hole or two down with only three or four to go, the very long putts would go down, and the pitches finish right beside the hole.

Dr A. Cleland (Sandy), amongst many distinctions, was our longest serving Captain, having been elected in 1938, served throughout the Second World War years until 1946. A general practitioner in Musselburgh and doctor to Loretto School, he tackled all the problems caused by the war with a stout heart, a cheerful manner, and very effectively. As can be imagined, the membership income dropped in a most alarming manner. Staff, both green and clubhouse, disappeared into the Forces or other war work; petrol, greenkeeping supplies and machinery were virtually unobtainable. Nevertheless, Sandy and his Committee, with the aid of the few remaining staff, kept the Club in the black and in good heart for recovery when the members came back.

It was a pretty close run thing at times such as the 1941 A.G.M. when he reported a surplus of income over expenditure of £17 17s 8d! Things improved financially from that time, largely due to very stringent economies being effected, and a lot of hard work and long hours put in. It was a great joy to get back to the course and find it in reasonable shape, thanks to their devoted stewardship. Probably the worst feature was the length and degree of encroachment of the rough, which made for slow play, as golf balls were very hard to come by then, and a lot of time was spent in diligent searching.

Sandy was a very useful golfer and he had a most friendly and welcoming manner which put new members at once at ease, and made guests feel at home. He and his wife, who had kept goal for Scotland at hockey, played frequently on the course. Quite often they played with a medical colleague from Musselburgh, Dr Laing and his wife. **Charles Laing** was a one-handed golfer, not due to any obvious infirmity, but caused by arthritis in one hand, which prevented him from holding the club properly. By practice and concentration he developed a very reasonable standard of play.

The Plaque with the Captains' names inscribed, placed above the fireplace, was presented to the Club by Sandy Cleland in 1953.

J. H. Carmichael (Jimmy), born in 1900, is an example of the sporting all-rounders who have always been found in number among our members. A keen Watsonian, he played rugby for them from 1919 to 1927, being Captain in the 1925-26 season, after gaining three International caps in 1921, and playing many times for Edinburgh in the Inter City. He was also a tennis player at the Waverley Club, although it is suggested that this might have been more for courting than serious tennis, as Vera Wood Hawks, sister of Victor, was a leading light there. They married in 1926 and had sixty-three years together before his death in 1990.

CHARACTERS ALL

GOLF CLUBS AND GOLFERS

The Quarry Hole from the Tee, showing guide flag.

J. D. LOWNIE, W.S.
Hon. Sec.

An Ex-Captain and Past Hon. Secretary, FRED MARSHALL.

The Captain and one of the best golfers in the Club, Dr A. CLELAND

Captain 1956-1957, A. SPOTTISWODE RITCHIE

CLAUDE N. MARSHALL, A very old Member

BERTIE PAUL, [Golfer and Conjuror]

T. A. GENTLES, K.C. A Member of the Senior G.S.

The famous Clubmaster, ALEC GLASGOW and his dog.

C. R. CROMBIE

HARRY NESS and a cigar.

GEORGE HAY, An ex-Member of Council

T. W. HARPER

LUFFNESS NEW GOLF CLUB—By "MEL"

Nineteen miles from Edinburgh, on the way to North Berwick, we come across the Luffness New Golf Club, one of the nicest clubs and courses in Scotland. The Club, which has a membership of 400 and a seven-years' waiting-list, was formed in 1894, the nucleus being the enrolment of 102 gentlemen to whom Life Membership was £6 each. Among them was the late Lord Balfour (then Mr. A. J. Balfour). The club-house, built in 1902, possesses one of the finest smoking-rooms to be found in any golf club, and it has been enlarged within the past three years. The course itself has beautiful springy seaside turf, like its neighbour, Gullane, and, apart from the sixth and seventh holes, is almost flat, yet full of character, and 70' is seldom broken. It is 6085 yards long, with a bogey of 75.' Alec, the club-master, is a great character, and has been connected with the Club since 1912, when he used to bring the victuals in a hand-cart to the Club

NEXT WEEK: ELIE GOLF CLUB, FIFE

69

Jimmy joined Luffness in December 1938, being also a member of Mortonhall, Gullane and Bruntsfield. He found Luffness much to his liking and very soon became a well-known and popular figure. Being a natural athlete, he was a very strong player with a low handicap and was an active and extremely able member of the Pirates' Golfing Society, in addition to being a member of other clubs such as the British Rugby Club of Paris, the Rugby Internationalists' Club and later the Seniors. He was elected Captain in April 1963 for the customary two years, and in recognition of his service to the Club and seniority, was invited to become an Honorary Member in November 1977. He was wont to remark that a round on his other courses was just a game of golf, whereas a day at Luffness was an outing.

He was a great enthusiast for cars, which he had driven right from attaining legal age. In these days before mass production, makes of cars and individual cars by the same makers had their own idiosyncrasies if not personalities. His new car was always the best he had ever had, and on one occasion, having replaced a very effective but quiet car with a more noisy and faster running one, drew

Statuette of Freddie Tait on the mantelpiece of Luffness New G.C. lounge.

the distinction that this one was a "Revver" and quite superior. Within a year or thereby this was in due course replaced by "the finest car he had ever had". He tended to be rather the same with his golf clubs, changing them with greater frequency than most, with the result that many of his friends and particularly brother-in-law, Victor Wood Hawks, were always equipped with the latest model available, *and* at bargain prices.

He presented the Club with the statuette of Freddie Tait that sits on the mantelpiece. The story goes that this caused about the only minor ripple on the placid surface of his sixty-three years of connubial bliss. The statuette was the property of his wife's family, and Jimmy, in a generous moment, carried away by his love and enthusiasm for Luffness, made the gift without any prior reference to the legal owner!

W. H. Stevenson (Billy) became a member in 1949 and was appointed Hon. Secretary very shortly after that to succeed John Lownie who was retiring after twenty years' service. In his early thirties at that time, he brought fresh ideas and new energy into the post and ran the affairs of the Club in a very efficient manner. He had an extremely genial personality and being present in the Clubhouse most weekends, was on very good terms with all, and was very effective in helping to arrange games and make sure that no-one was left out. Nothing was a bother to him, and he took the secretarial duties in his effortless stride.

At that time the secretarial work was done in his C.A. firm's office and apart from paying the wages and issuing and collecting score cards on Medal days, no action took place at the Club. Among his innovations was a card system for membership and a loose-leaf Minute Book into which all the material was typed, as opposed to a solid ruled book with all entries handwritten, in varying skills of calligraphy. This indeed was a vast improvement, much appreciated by subsequent researchers such as the contributors to this volume.

Many members and probably quite a few guests will have noticed the green pane of glass in the bottom left hand corner of the middle section of the long west-facing window of the lounge. This was a replacement for a pane broken by a wild shot off the first tee shortly after Billy had taken office. As it was just after the war, fancy glass was still in short supply and the local joiner was quite unable to produce a piece of glass anywhere near the pattern of the other panes. The nearest he could offer, other than plain glass, was a rather dark green pane with a pronounced pattern on it. Billy, seeing that it had at least some form of pattern, and wanting to get the job done quickly, gave his approval, and the deed was done. Being green/red colour blind, he did not realise that it stuck out like the proverbial sore thumb, until the members ribbed him about it the next weekend. Somewhat red faced, he was keen to get it replaced as soon as suitable glass became available, but the Committee reckoned it provided a bit of character to the window, and it was resolved to leave it there until it got broken again. One member gave it the name "The W. H. Stevenson Memorial Window", and thus it has remained. Although somewhat chipped and cracked, it was never broken. In 1992 when a new frame and glass were installed along with double glazing of the other lounge windows, it was glazed with plain clear glass, but it was arranged that the bottom left hand pane would be of tinted glass to perpetuate the "Memorial" to a very popular and efficient Secretary.

John Graham, Captain 1968-70, was the initiator of the annual matches against the Barbadians from Royal St George's at Sandwich, as is described in Peter Tassell's contribution. As our Captain, he was a member of the first combined side from Gullane, Luffness and Muirfield, called "The Prestonpansies", organised by Gordon Kerr of the Honourable Company, to go down to Sandwich for a return match. This was a two-day encounter, played over a Saturday and Sunday—two 18-hole matches of foursome play each day.

The Men's Lounge there is a very fine example of what pertains in

71

an all-male club, and is furnished rather like a traditional Officers' Mess, with long dark red leather settees, set in an open square in front of the big open fire, with a brass "bum warmer" round it. Above all this is a magnificent board or plaque with St George and the Dragon carved on the top of it with the captains' names recorded below. It starts in 1887 with the Earl of Wincheslea, followed by a succession of the aristocracy and titled gentry, with more than a sprinkling of the highest ranking leaders of our armed forces, reaching a peak in the mid-thirties with HRH The Prince of Wales. When John first saw this formidable list, he remarked: "Cor! This makes the Honourable Company look like Craigentinny."

It is a marvellous experience to take part in any of these matches whether home or away, as they are played between congenial characters entirely for fun, with the final result not being of world-shattering importance. The away games are quite hard work with at least four rounds in two days, very often six in three, or even eight in four, when the visitor wants to extract the maximum value for the long trip there and back. In the opinion of any member who has taken part in any of these matches, establishing the Barbadian match was his finest and longest standing contribution to the history of this Club.

John Graham made his mark on the Club in many other ways including carpeting in the Clubhouse. All facets of his office were conducted most efficiently and with the greatest good humour.

There are probably more tales about **John Leckie** than any other member and the following anecdotes are absolutely true. John came to Luffness at the end of 1944 from the West where he had learned his golf in a very hard school on such links as Old Troon and Prestwick. He was a very keen member, always with the best interests of the Club at heart. He represented the Club in the County Cup on several occasions and his name is on many of the trophies, and he was an enthusiastic supporter of the Club Dinner matches from the very start. His turnout was always immaculate, usually favouring light coloured plus fours with a fawn cardigan and a cap of a light hue as well. His golf was of such a calibre that, even in these days, his white shoes passed without comment.

There might be some members from the fifties to mid-seventies, when he was most active, who might suggest that John was maybe in the back row when senses of humour were being issued. Be that as it may, any less than perfect shots executed by John were due to some outside agency. For instance, while playing his second shot one winter to the 7th green, he duffed it, and the ball stopped well short of the green. He attributed this lapse to his scarf blowing over his eyes as he played his stroke, to which one of his opponents remarked, "You will have to do better than that, John, you took it off while playing the 4th!" On another occasion in the early seventies, he was playing the second shot at the 14th, when at the top of his backswing, a cow on the grazings to the right of the fairway made a loud bellow and John played one of his rare poor shots. Frustrated and furious, he addressed his playing companions saying, "Did you hear that bloody cow? It deliberately went 'MOO' at the top of my backswing. The Club should never have allowed stock on that land."

He was a keen and successful Dinner Match player and, on one occasion, when he and his partner had been strongly fancied, and went down to defeat most unexpectedly, not entirely due to his partner's shortcomings or the brilliance of the opposition, he attributed this failure to the mischance that he had brought his medal set of clubs instead of his matchplay ones. Another contributor recalls that his first Dinner Match on joining the Club was with John as partner and that he was ordered to the 1st tee and was told that John Leckie would play the "executive" shots. The drive landed well down in the middle of the fairway to John's satisfaction. He then played the "executive" shot to the green, which it overshot substantially. John apologised for forgetting that he had been told it was a new ball they were playing! He took the ribbing in good part, even to the extent that when matches were being called at a certain dinner, one punter instead of calling "Five bob on Smith" or "Five bob on my partner", called "Five bob against Leckie"—the first instance of aggressive betting.

His wife's delicate health required a more benign climate than the Lothians, and he moved to Lanzarote in the early seventies. He made available his long experience to that club in their early days when establishing a course on virtually a lunar landscape with, at that time, scant supplies of water. He still returned to Luffness for a couple of months or so every summer, when he was warmly welcomed as a long lost friend.

J. D. W. Spence (Jack) was elected to the Committee in 1962 when his expertise in catering and accountancy was of great value to the Club, and he became Captain in 1971. He was an exemplary holder of this office, but this has no bearing on his inclusion in this section. Jack was a polio victim with severe disablement of his legs, requiring metal callipers, leather braces and straps, and two sticks to walk with. He never let this handicap interfere with his game or cause any embarrassment to his playing companions, and he always kept his place on the course, regardless of the personal physical effort it cost him. He was a keen competitor in the Dinner Matches—and in those days one was unpopular if one did not get round in under two and a half hours.

In the coldest days in winter he would have no more than two thin cardigans on, and such was the effort he required to make that he never felt cold. He would walk to his ball with his two sticks, hand them to his faithful caddie, "Cubbie", in exchange for his club, balance himself, hit a very serviceable shot and get his sticks back again. Despite his physical shortcomings, he was a very steady golfer and his name can be found on our handicap trophy lists. He was never known to complain or suggest that his four was going too fast for him. He just got stuck into his task and kept smiling.

He had another favourite sport which he could enjoy, despite his legs, and that was canoeing, which he did on the north-west coast. He would tackle quite prodigious distances in quite rough conditions that one hundred per cent fit mortals would think twice about. He revelled in this sport as his upper body was virtually unaffected, and he had developed enormous strength in his torso and arms, and this was an area in which he could hold his own with anyone.

David Lawrie comes into this same category, alas, a victim of birth deformities severely affecting his left arm, which for all practical purposes was almost useless. As a result he played golf with his right hand only, and to such sterling effect as to be Champion of the Society of One-Armed Golfers in 1965, 1968 and 1976. He too was a very keen Dinner Match player, and it was always better to be his partner than in opposition. He had developed an enormously strong right arm, wrist and hand which, combined with his own brand of concentration, could strike the ball as far and straighter than most of his two-handed contemporaries. A most accurate putter, he was capable of holing out time and again with his own special large headed putter, when the pressure was really on. A more cheerful delightful companion for a game of golf one could not find, and he never let his infirmities intrude in his way of life, on or off the course.

In the totally inexplicable way that life works, David was stricken with cancer when still in his forties, and, despite a heroic and unremitting fight against it, he finally succumbed in 1985. He had several courses of long and painful treatment from which he would return to Luffness somewhat hairless and weakened, and take up where he had left off, still with a cheery smile. It was always a joy to share his company. His memory is kept alive for ever in the form of the Memorial Fountain, behind the 10th tee, which bears an inscription recalling his feats.

Among current members **Stanley Mayer** must be one of our most distinguished performers, certainly in the senior ranks. Although only becoming a member on retiral in 1985, he has made his mark by being Club Champion in 1989, the same year that he won the Winter Foursomes with John MacNeil as partner. Learning his golf at Eastwood, he first came to the fore as a student at Glasgow University, when he won the Scottish Universities' Championship in 1943 and 1945. This success brought him the honour of captaining the Scottish Students against their English counterparts at St Andrews in the first match of this series, inaugurated just after the end of World War II. It is satisfactory to record that he led his side to a resounding victory. Around this period as an individual, he was the first winner of the Boyd Quaich, open to students world wide. He also played County golf for Renfrewshire and in District matches for the West of

Scotland. Later, while living and teaching in Wiltshire, he won the County Championship several times and was a regular player for the County. Coming back to Scotland saw him win the Courtauld Thomson Trophy at Gullane in 1960. Settling in his profession in Galashiels, he became Club Champion at Torwoodlee and a prominent force in Borders golf. The formation of the Scottish Schools' Golf Association owes a lot to the enthusiasm of a small group of teachers, of which he was one, in the Lothians and Borders. He became President of the Association, which has proved successful in encouraging young golfers.

Since joining Luffness his most notable performance was winning the Scottish Amateur Seniors' Championship in 1989. His score of 72+67=139 established a record low aggregate, so far unbeaten. Current handicap 4—not bad for a septuagenarian!

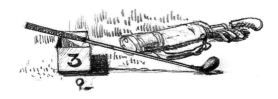

"I love everything that is old: old friends; old times; old manners; old books; old wines."—Goldsmith.

A former Captain's wife was bitten by Mr Glasgow's bull mastiff—she bit it back.

"Winning is not everything—it is the only thing."—Colin Chapman.

THE THURSDAY CLUB

This institution, so very popular amongst today's geriatric members, had its origin in the 1950s from the gathering together on their half day of some doctors and their friends including George and Alex Cochrane, Sandy Cleland, Charles Laing, Leslie Stewart, Tom Torrance and K. Paterson-Brown. The latter had the distinction of recording a 77 at the age of 79 in 1972, nine years before his death.

As people retired earlier and life expectancy increased, coupled with more Edinburgh members moving to East Lothian on retiral, the numbers have increased enormously over the last decade or so. It is not uncommon for over thirty members to turn up and be organised into fours by drawing a numbered tee from a mug. Play is by foursomes naturally, on handicap, and since inception the stakes have been 15 pence outward half, 15 pence inward, 20 pence on the game, total individual liability 50 pence. Spurred on by such high stakes, competition is intense! The draw takes place while members are enjoying an aperitif before lunch. As the fours are made up they go in to lunch and either toss up at the table or elect to "throw the balls up" at the 1st tee to decide the pairings. The various fours sort themselves into order of play, some electing to have a shorter round and play from the 5th tee, some playing from 1st to 12th, a few not even reaching the "starting line"! There is never any argument, and even in the shorter afternoons of midwinter there is never any need to have a formal starting order. In the last decade or so, such stalwarts as John Allan, George Harland, ''Bal'' Hendry, Sydney Newman, Graham and Donald Sandison, Kitchy White and ''Geordie'' Williamson epitomise the spirit of the Thursday Club.

Of recent years Geoffrey Thomson has been the chief organiser who arranges it all with the utmost good humour and tact, and manages to satisfy the diverse wishes from a wide span of ages and physical ability to cope with a full or shortened round. Should he not be available, there are always one or two reserves who willingly take on this task, which ensures a very happy day for all.

Matches are played on a Home and Away basis with the golfers of the Gullane G.C. Seniors.

March 31st, 1952—Members' Guests 2/6; Visiting Clubs' Temporary Membership 6/- on Weekdays and 15/- on Saturdays and Sundays.

1954—Caddies—Men were 7/6 a round and Boys were 5/- per round.

THE THREEPENNY CLUB

by

RONNIE PAUL

In the early 'thirties the old threepenny piece was used in the following manner. All who wished to participate (including "hangers-on") collected their threepenny pieces throughout the week. At the weekend they would deposit these on a table in the Smoking Room at Luffness and they were used to pay for the drinks. At a later date it was decided to utilise the "table top collection" to allow those concerned to have an annual weekend away, playing golf at the Goswick Course (just south of Berwick-on-Tweed). The six regular subscribers were Bertie Paul (Honorary Secretary), Claude Marshall, Tommy Gentles, K.C., Ernest Millar, Harry Ness and Harry Wakelin, and they plus others would set off by train (the "Flying Scotsman" no less!). As this was the London train they had to bribe the train driver and the guard to stop at the insignificant Goswick Station on its journey south. Incredible as it may seem the same train would pick them up on its return journey north. What went on during this outing is a matter for conjecture; suffice it to say that the caddies were all of the female species. Could it be that they were the forerunners of Faldo's Fanny Sunesson and Sandy Lyle's second wife?

Assuming that all this money was expended on the journey south, the drinks at Luffness still had to be paid, and a lottery was brought into use for this purpose. The brass ash trays, still in use today, were made and donated by Bertie Paul, and each had a black painted nick on the rim which, after spinning had stopped, would point fairly and squarely at the individual who would have the doubtful pleasure of paying for the drinks.

The ash trays, even today, could fulfil this same function if the tables were glass-topped and the ash trays were re-ground so as to provide a spinning point on the base again. Alas, the standards of workmanship have deteriorated, and so the tables and the ash trays no longer function as intended.

The clock, still in use today, and placed above the entrance to the Smoke Room, was presented by John Paul, the brother of Bertie. Rumour has it that *his* gesture was prompted because he had no desire to be up-staged by his brother.

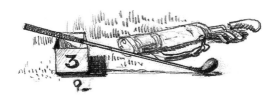

On showing slight displeasure about a wayward shot a player actually threw his club in disgust and was curtly reprimanded and told to pay a fine to charity. "No way," responded the culprit, "that was only a mini-throw."

A CHAMPION DRIVE?

CLUB CHAMPIONS

1980	R. E. Simpson
1981	J. R. Inglis
1982	J. R. Inglis
1983	J. R. Inglis
1984	J. R. Inglis
1985	D. L. Murray
1986	C. Cuthbert
1987	C. Cuthbert
1988	C. Cuthbert
1989	A. S. Mayer
1990	C. Cuthbert
1991	I. Smith
1992	C. Cuthbert
1993	I. Smith

MUST BE A DINNER GAME

CLUB DINNERS

by

TOM SCOTT and CAMERON MILLER

A proposal that Club Dinners be introduced was first submitted by the Committee at the Annual General Meeting held on 14 February 1955 and was approved unanimously. A small Sub-Committee was set up to make the necessary arrangements, and a Recorder, Tom Scott, was appointed. The Sub-Committee recommended that Dinner Matches be played, as foursomes only, over 18 or 36 holes, on a handicap basis, and with a stake of 10/-, with the players and other interested parties able to place side-stakes on each match. No limit was placed on the number of such stakes, but the amount of each side-stake was restricted to a unit of 5/-. The duty of the Recorder, as his title indicated, was to keep details of all matches entered into, and arrange settlements of all sums won and lost. It was recommended that members attending a dinner should assemble in the lounge of the Clubhouse about 45 minutes before dining to arrange matches and register these with the Recorder on a standard prepared card. After dinner the Recorder would read out details of each match, indicating the stroke differential, and the diners would then place their side bets accordingly. These recommendations were accepted by the Committee of the Club.

The first Club dinner was held on 22 October 1955 in the Royal British Hotel, Edinburgh. Two further dinners were held at the same venue in 1956. A fourth dinner which had been arranged for January 1957 was postponed because of petrol rationing, and was subsequently held on 3 May 1957 in the Clubhouse. These early dinners had been well supported with about 30 members present on each occasion. In June, the Committee decided to hold dinners quarterly, using the Clubhouse for all except the January dinner. The Committee also decided to hire a bus to take members from Edinburgh to Luffness and return. 1960-61 showed a diminishing demand for places at the dinner, but since that time there has been growing support for the venture, and on a number of occasions there has been a waiting list. The practice of holding the winter dinner in town was discontinued many years ago.

The dinners at Luffness Clubhouse today follow a routine pattern—dress formal (dinner jacket and black tie). The arrival of the bus signifies the start of the period of pre-dinner activity during which challenges are made and accepted. These may lead to some of the most incongruous pairings of what must appear to be the most incompatible individuals in the Club. Be that as it may, the games are entered on the requisite card with the handicaps of those involved, and handed to the Recorder, who duly establishes the stroke differential and which side will receive or give strokes. This bartering, which usually lasts some 40 minutes, ends when the dining room door is opened and the Secretary declares ''Dinner is served'', the response to which is a rush to acquire seats for yourself and your friends, yet another visit to ''tidy up'', or total inability to recognise what has been said. Members take their places at a number of tables of four to six persons. The Captain has his own table in the centre of the room to which the new first dinner members, the Secretary, the Recorder and others of the Captain's choice are invited. Grace precedes each dinner. The following was delivered by Eddie Foote on one occasion:

Oh Thou who made the greens and sand
The fairways and the rough,
For all the blessings of Thy hand
Our thanks are scarce enough.
Now sit and join us, Lord of all,
And share with us Thy grace
For those who swipe the small white ball
Make glad within this place.

An excellent meal prepared by the Clubmaster's wife, accompanied by copious libations of wine, is followed by the Loyal Toast proposed by the Captain, who, indicating that this is no time for formal speeches, inevitably goes on to provide the assembled group with an oration which he is determined to deliver whether it is acceptable or not. These may, on some occasions, be succinct and humorous. At this time the biscuits, cheese and port have been consumed and those present slowly drift to the lounge to acquire liqueurs and coffee, while others utilise the break to relieve themselves of any unnecessary stress or strain before settling down for the penultimate part of the evening, namely the calling of the games. The seats are arranged in such a way that all have full view of the Recorder, who, sitting in the centre of the room, with the doubtful assistance of the Secretary and Captain, revel in their moment of glory, floodlit as they are, and proceed to call the matches. The basic stake is one of £2 for each individual. Nobody is permitted to place bets on his own game, but he is free to, and frequently cajoled into accepting bets from others. Although the side bets are restricted to 25p it is quite surprising how many show a total disinterest in responding, even when their parentage may be seriously challenged. The business is usually both speedy and efficient and normally allows all matches to be called. To conclude the evening a Vote of Thanks to the Recorder is the indication that those present should prepare for the return journey home and finish off their drinks. Finding the bus some 30 minutes later can be an almost unsurmountable task for some. For those with cars driven by their long suffering wives, the stony silence which greets them is often quite impossible to bear.

The Recorders have to be made of stern stuff to cope with the quick-fire patter which emanates from the mouths of the ''players'' who all too frequently exhibit the signs, and alas, all too often elicit the symptoms of a wide range of inebriate manifestations. Tom Scott, Derek Stewart, Hamish Steven, George Low, Peter Clark and Mike Livingston have all battled nobly over the years in these confrontations. On most occasions the odds are very heavily against them.

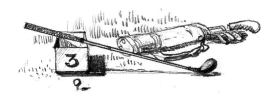

DINNER MATCHES

At ev'ry Dinner Match I've thought that I would surely win:
My own performance really ought to bring the money in.
I've seldom played, in any Match, a less than perfect shot;
But were my partners up to scratch? Well, frankly, they were not.
A partner with a handicap of even two or three
Does little to preserve the gap 'twixt bankruptcy and me.
At first, I could not follow quite why I so often lost.
And, as I lay in bed at night, I counted up the cost:
My drives are a delight to see; my irons are supreme;
My putting pleases even me; my chipping is a dream.
Then suddenly there dawned on me a point I'd overlooked,
Explaining why, 'twas plain to see, my foursomes goose was cooked.

Spectators never could deny that ev'ry shot I struck,
Tho' perfect, was attended by incredibly bad luck.
A guide-post that was not a guide; a green that was too small;
A partner who would not provide a decent make of ball.
A seagull wheeling in the air; a ball not running true;
A bunker that should not be there, to mention but a few.
(Tho', when I contemplate a trap, I take the decent view:
It's there to keep my handicap at twenty-four point two.)
I carry partners on my back, until my back is sore;
I bravely face misfortune's flak. I suffer more and more.
At times I'm almost on the brink of giving golf a miss.
I watch my partner's swing, and think ''No money-spinner this!''
So why do I continue thus to wear the martyr's crown?
And never make the slightest fuss when partners let me down?
It isn't for my gentle charm, my disposition sweet,
That fellow members twist my arm, and press me to compete.
It's not a model they require, although I'm proud to state
My swing is what they all admire, and strive to imitate.
Alas! the reason's more mundane, as you perhaps have sensed;
They've found in me, it's very plain, the man to play against.

Cameron Miller.

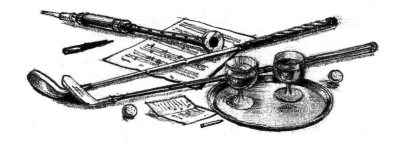

LUFFNESS LINKS

Blythe hae I been on Elie Links,
Blythe hae I been near Berwick Law
The braes of Gullane please me weel,
But Luffness Links are best o' a'.

O'er Gullane Hill and Gullane Braes
The wastlin breezes saftly blaw,
There mony happy 'oors I've spent,
But Luffness Links are best o' a'.

North Berwick too hath mony charms,
Frae ''Garry Point'' to o'er the wa',
''Perfection Hole'' and ''Schipka Pass'',
But Luffness Links are best o' a'.

The wide expanse alang the hill,
Wi' bunkers neither few nor sma',
The views o'er Aberlady Bay,
Mak' Luffness Links the best o' a'.

Luffness Links and double drinks
And members' guests are cantie-o,
They'll ne'er forget the day we met
Upon the Links o' Luffness-o!

To the tune of Corn Riggs   *by A. Gilmour and A. H. White*
—with acknowledgements to Mr R. Burns,
late of Dumfries.

THE 1ST TEE IS CLOSE TO THE CLUBHOUSE
(OFTEN TOO CLOSE)

OF GUESTS

by

W. DONALD MacLENNAN

Luffness New is justifiably proud of the hospitality which it extends throughout the year to all who share their love of the game of golf which is essentially physical but demands at the same time such a complex and unique response psychologically—always challenging, frequently infuriating, satisfying when accompanied by success, and so utterly and completely frustrating when it is not. Who would believe that the process of guiding a small ball through a series of natural and man-made hazards from tee to green, finally to despatch it into a small hole, would evoke so many different responses? Some, with justification, may well feel that their hitherto impeccable life styles have been replaced by bizarre behavioural patterns which are both primitive and moronic. For others there is hollow comfort in the fact that they react so diabolically to circumstances which seem to them to be heavily loaded against them even before they start to play. Be that as it may the vast majority really do enjoy the game and return to the links whenever they can.

Visiting Clubs are an increasing source of revenue. Many have been returning for years and include small and large parties such as the Royal Colleges G.C.; Barclays Bank; the Blackford Golf Club; the All Spheres and the W.S. Society, both essentially members of the legal fraternity; the Barbadians, Dr Langland's Party; The British Rugby Club of Paris; the East Lothian Farmers; the Wedgers; the Honourable

Company of Rutland Golfers; East Lothian Police and the Pirates. Some warrant further comment.

The British Rugby Club of Paris (Scottish Section) was founded in 1926 by D. S. Carmichael, who presented the original cup for competition. The criteria for membership are somewhat vague. Involvement in rugby football and golf are viewed with favour, while any additional connection with Paris, however tenuous, may help to carry the day.

J. H. Carmichael succeeded his father from 1948-50, the Club having been inactive during the Second World War. G. B. Hendry (Bal) was responsible for reviving the B.R.C.P. in 1948, and later became their Captain in 1956. The third generation of the Carmichaels—J. J. was Captain in 1980—surely a unique trio from one family, and who knows there may be more to come?

Many Luffness New members have held office over the years. There can be no doubt that they always enjoy their visits to Luffness New.

The W.S. Golf Club was founded in 1957 at the instigation of Sir Hugh Watson, a distinguished Deputy Keeper of the Signet, and Royal High School Scholar. The inaugural meeting was held in the Signet Library on 2 December. The first Captain was Ewan B. Robertson, a current member of Luffness New. This was indeed to herald a long and happy relationship with Luffness. Since 1960 the Club's Annual Outing to our course has been unbroken. In that year forty members attended and James H. A. McKenzie, another member, won the afternoon Stableford Foursomes Competition.

It is interesting to note that the gratuity paid that year to the staff at Luffness was £2 which is less than the current price of a Luffness gin and tonic. Inflation has a great deal to answer for!

Members of Luffness have continued to appear on the W.S. prize list, e.g. John Marshall, a Past Luffness New Captain, won the Deputy Keeper's Quaich in 1963.

A Minute of the Club's Annual Meeting paints a picture which epitomises the spirit which exists between our respective clubs—"At the Luffness Outing H. J. L. Allan retained the Deputy Keeper's Quaich with a score of 78–13=65. After lunch, when the usual Stableford Competition had begun, a rain storm broke, making two nations of us—the wets, who were caught up on distant fairways, and the drys who had not strayed from the purlieus of the Clubhouse. The latter thereupon repaired to the Smoking Room where they carried a motion that the sweepstake should be annulled, and settled back to enjoy the efforts of those outside engaged in the quest for a vanished El Dorado. To the best scorer (whose card was excellent in the conditions) the Secretary was permitted to minister a goblet of brandy by way of a sop."

The Pirates were formed in 1926—a club whose aim was to encourage foursomes golf and camaraderie. A. D. F. Torrance (Tony) was instrumental in encouraging his brother William to create the Pirates, and they play at a number of East Lothian courses including Gullane, Longniddry, Luffness New and Muirfield. Their 50th Anniversary Meeting was held at Luffness New, when they presented the Club with two decanters to mark the occasion. They are used at the Club dinners. Sandy Cleland was a devoted member of the Pirates, as was Tom Scott.

The Royal Colleges Golf Club has been coming to Luffness since 1923. The first Captain was Dr Douglas Argyll Robertson, an excellent golfer in his own right. He was a Founder Member of the Luffness New Golf Club and played in the first competition held there. Today some 60 physicians and surgeons descend on the course on the May Holiday, psyched up to partake in the morning medal round and in the afternoon in the annual match between the Surgeons and the Physicians in a series of level foursomes matches. In the evening 42-44 remain to partake of dinner in the Clubhouse. This is followed by a report from the Recorder who is given considerable licence to read his personal comments on the events of the previous year. These are normally highly amusing, but there can be a disaster when one is confronted by someone who, though well intentioned, is totally lacking in humour, and very often cannot read his own writing. John Savin wrote an excellent article in the *British Medical Journal* based on previous reports by Recorders, large excerpts from which are generously provided.

"When the great day dawns members of the Club leave for Luffness, confident that juniors will 'cover their absence with a skill derived from frequent practice', the battle of the status symbols begins on the roads. Once the surgeons had the bulkier cars. Then the tide turned in 1957—'chauffeur-driven limousines of the physicians were followed at a discrete distance by the second-hand tumbrels of the surgeons, who were obviously elated to park in such distinguished company'. Sheltered parking spaces have been in demand since 1951 when a drive from the first tee 'bagged a gynaecological Bentley and an orthopaedic Super Snipe before coming to rest under a medical A40'. Nowadays, of course, members of both colleges drive small family saloons.

Traditionally the weather is fine. 'The sun shone, the birds sang, and the gentle east wind made ideal conditions' chirruped one Recorder. An occasional squall is allowed, often blowing up without even a call of 'Fore' from the Almighty. Less often 'the flamboyant sweaters, the esoteric shirts and the polychromatic pants, dear to the hearts of the highly handicapped, are hidden under windjammers and rubber breeks'. The Recorders often comment on members' clothing which can range from 'immaculate consulting attire' to 'a blue jersey borrowed from some obese fisherman'. Perhaps the most mysterious garment was a set of plus fours of Swiss manufacture: 'The main talking point was the three zip fasteners whch ensure that all things are possible, and in any direction.' All manner of decoys are used to put off opponents and team-mates alike, such is the high degree of egotism of all concerned, and their desire to impress whatsoever the cost. The 'surgeons have a penchant for wearing "pus coloured caps" for example, and one gamesman was even said to have a tame moth which he had trained to fly out of his socks as proof that he was lacking in practice'.

In 1951 trolleys arrived to replace the human caddies who, until then, had the effect of at least deflating egos. 'A hefty surgeon sadly surveying his largest divot was brusquely told to "tak it hame and practise on it". Another who had "dwelt long enough in the rough" heard his caddy mutter "it's a ferret he's needin', no' a caddy". Another, finding his ball in a rut on the road crossing the 15th fairway, tried to ignore his caddy's bright suggestion to avoid a penalty lift—"pee on it an' ca' it casual water". Then there was the occasion when "a surgeon's trolley joined him in a sand trap at the 15th and then upset". His Calvinistic partner added 13 strokes to his score for grounding his clubs in the bunker.'

The 'rosy and well groomed' surgeons enjoy thrashing the physicians. Friendly banter may cause cracks to appear in a member's 'brittle gentlemanly veneer'. One successful competitor long before Trevino was able to use his vocal chords 'right up to the moment of impact', while another less successful one had a partner who was 'the reverse of a ventriloquist in that he said nothing, but his lips moved'.

The Recorder's comments are seldom designed to encourage—'one member performed strange fertility rites, waving his club like a magic wand and thereby assisting the wind pollination of the East Lothian flora'.

The evening dinner in the Clubhouse is informal. While the surgeons normally 'scrub up before dinner', the physicians are less punctilious in this matter. 'Few even bother to change their socks.' 'Most obey Timothy's maxim to drink no longer water but use a little wine for thy stomach's sake' but supply their own medical excuses. Surgeons like to 'arrange their own anaesthesia' or 'use alcohol to achieve inner cleanliness and sterilisation of the gut'. The few physicians, like Bernard Shaw, drink only to make other people more interesting.''

All good things come to an end and the light of morning will see all those professional gentlemen back to the wards—yesterday is already a day in the past, and next year is too far away to give it much of a thought.

References

British Rugby Club of Paris (Scottish Section) — Personal comments from G. B. Hendry.

W.S. Golf Club — Personal comments from G. A. Henry.

The Royal Colleges Golf Club — 1890-1990 — *Brit. Med. Journal*, Dec. 1990, vol. 301, 1462-1463. John A. Savin.

ANTIGUANS v. BARBADIANS

by

BRYAN (Peter) TASSELL

1994 sees the centenary of the Club: it also sees the twenty-fifth match between the Antiguans of Luffness and the Barbadians of Royal St George's.

As this book will be read when those alive today are no longer present to give evidence, it seems right to set out how this contest began and why its teams were so called.

In the winter of 1969/70 the writer received a letter from John Graham, then Captain, saying that he had heard that the writer's party were again coming to East Lothian in the coming spring and that, if this was so, would they care to play a match against Luffness. His offer was immediately and warmly accepted and a date fixed.

During the correspondence the point was made in a telephone conversation that the visiting party, though composed of members of Royal St George's was in no sense representing the Club, but was merely an association of equal numbers of older and younger members who met a few times each winter for foursomes and the pleasures of the table. "Do you have a name?" asked John. "Why yes, we have," was the reply. "We call ourselves the Barbadians because we never go there in the winter—a sort of W. S. Gilbert inversion if you follow me." "Indeed I do," said John, "Excellent! We'll call ourselves the Antiguans: I've just had a holiday there but I don't expect I'll ever go again. Will that marry up?" It most certainly did, and in this style was the first match fixed. Accordingly on Saturday, 2 May 1970, fourteen Barbadians walked through the front door of the Luffness Clubhouse to be welcomed by John Graham and thirteen Antiguans. With one exception there was not a member of either side who had previously met a member of the other side. There was a little pause as the introductions were made, and we smiled cheerfully at each other and then, suddenly and spontaneously the whole thing seemed to light up, and the light has never gone out. Throughout all the years there has been a special warmth in our meetings. To Barbadians as they cross the threshold each spring it is like coming home.

Accurate results of all the matches are recorded in the Barbadians' record books which show that between 1970 and 1993, twenty-four matches were played. The Barbadians won twelve, the Antiguans won nine and three were halved. They are, however, brought alive by innumerable photographs from friendly cameras. From these prints far from gloomy faces look out from sunlit tees and greens, from smoking room and from dining room, in golfing garb, in dinner jacket and in Highland evening dress; and, year after year, from that mobile haven in the shelter of the buckthorn by the ninth green which fortifies them for the homeward voyage and by its fountain evokes a tear, albeit a happy tear, for David Lawrie. Long-forgotten dramatic and comic events are recalled to each of us as we browse over the books, but only three have found their laconic way on to the paper, viz: in the opening match in 1970 Godfrey Ralli and Walter Brice went round in 74 to beat Alan Anderson and Geoffrey Thomson; in 1981 Hamish Steven and Bill MacLennan went one better with a 73 when beating Bobby Furber and John Reeves; and in 1972 Douglas Henderson holed the 16th in one when partnering Iain Mackenzie against Donald Smith and David Fison.

Over the years the match has grown. Beginning at 14-a-side it settled, after some early fluctuations, at 12-a-side through to 1978 since when it has steadily increased to 22-a-side in 1991, reduced to 20-a-side in 1992 and so intended in 1993. The governing factor has of course been the size of the Barbadians' touring party, to whom it has been a source of much pride that their hosts at Luffness, Muirfield and Gullane have each and all made it plain that any reasonable increase in their numbers will be welcome. On the Barbadian side the unique joys of the tour are so well known that many more would like to come, but experience suggests that 18- to 20-a-side may well be a sensible and manageable number.

It was in 1979, in the Captaincy of Donald Sandison, on the advocacy of James Falconer and Buster Wallace and with the approval of Bob Gardiner—Donald Sandison's predecessor in office, that the happy practice of both sides dining together at Luffness on the eve of the match was instituted and it has become an established custom ever since. On that first occasion the effect on the golf next day was dramatic, for the Barbadians, down by two matches to six at lunch, suffered almost total destruction in the afternoon, losing seven matches out of eight, their sole winner being Duncan Smith and Richard Tassell who got home on the last green against the Captain and Robin Carlyle. It would seem, however, that the Barbadians learnt from this hospitable hangover, the records showing that since 1978 they have had a little the better of the post-lunch argument, even on the occasion when one of their most experienced members performed the remarkable feat of lowering ten Bloody Marys before settling to the table.

The expenses of our mutual jollities have of course been shared in all the matches between the Antiguans and the Barbadians. In view of the four-figure sums which each side now cheerfully fields per annum as their share, the following sentence in the Barbadian ''Manager'''s letter to his sixteen fellow tourists after the 1972 tour must provoke a thought or two: ''The total cost of the Luffness Day, including a present of £10 to the Steward and his wife was £120 and I have paid our share of £60 to John Graham.'' There was of course no dinner.

Antiguans v. Barbadians.

Antiguans v. Barbadians Dinner—1992, in the Clubhouse.

Left to right: Jim Snow, Captain, Luffness New G.C.; Hamish Buchan, Captain, Gullane G.C.; Nigel Richardson, Vice-Captain, Luffness New G.C.; Lt.-Col. J. G. Tedford, Secretary, Luffness New G.C.; Garth Morrison, H.C.E.G.; Brian (Peter) Tassell, Royal St George G.C., "Manager" of the Barbadians.

Finally a word about the weather. Save for a few occasions in early May the match has always been played in April, yet in all the twenty-four matches from 1970 to 1993 inclusive every single game has been played out. This may of course indicate the firmness of purpose of the players but it is also evidence that the weather has never been intolerable. And indeed the comments in the records more than confirm this. It is true that on 1 May 1982 a sudden snowstorm out of a clear blue sky turned the whole links white at 1 p.m., but the snow knew its place and quietly melted away while we were lunching and all was green again by 2 o'clock. By contrast there are many more years of warmth and sunshine. Perhaps in our memory of happy days it is always, as in 1991, ''Cloudless blue sky—dawn to dusk''.

Golf etiquette—If you cannot say anything ''nice'' about your opponents—keep your mouth shut.

DOGS ARE NOT ALLOWED ON THE COURSE

CLUB SECRETARIES

1894-1903	J. Reid
1903-1909	J. I. Gillespie
1909-1919	R. C. Anderson
1919-1927	F. Marshall
1927-1929	C. G. Manford
1929-1949	J. D. Lownie
1949-1967	W. H. Stevenson
1967-1972	J. W. Oswald
1972-1973	P. Whyte
1973-1983	J. C. Falconer
1983-1985	A. Hogg
1985-1986	R. S. Murray
1986-19	J. G. Tedford

"FAMILY TICKETS ARE OBTAINABLE FROM THE CLUBMASTER"

CLUBMASTERS/CLUBMISTRESSES

1901- ?	Miss E. L. Purcell
1912-1938	A. L. Glasgow and Miss "Bunty" Thomson
1939-1945	Mr and Mrs W. Gilchrist
1945-1954	Mr and Mrs P. I. Jamieson
1955-1965	Mr and Mrs J. N. Gourlay
1965-1967	Mrs J. N. Gourlay
1967-1974	Mr and Mrs J. C. E. Scotland
1974-1982	Mr and Mrs E. C. Gilligan
1983-1985	Mr and Mrs A. C. Guthrie
1985-1987	Mr and Mrs G. Foreman
1987-19	Mr and Mrs J. J. Little

THE PREVAILING WIND IS FROM THE WEST!

LUFFNESS—A COURSE FOR ALL SEASONS

by

HECTOR BRYSON CHAWLA

As every member of every inland golf course knows, winter is that time of year when fairways turn into quagmires, bunkers into water holes and greens turn out to be forbidden territory for anyone actually wanting to putt.

With all this dampness underfoot we might be forgiven for thinking that things would be worse down the coast with a depression from somewhere out there transferring most of the North Sea briefly to somewhere up there. Not so. The sky may weep over Edinburgh but it smiles over Luffness, for some reason which defies the laws of weather forecasting.

In all conscience, these laws are strange enough as the French have long recognised. Whilst delivering their own weather reports with panache and scientific detail, they acquire this information by witchcraft. Before satellites circling the earth got it all wrong, their source of information was a frog, domiciled on a window sill in the Quai d'Orsay that danced to a different rhythm with every change of atmospheric pressure. Its pirouettes and gyrations were then translated into millibars for national distribution and to my knowledge, the frog always got it right.

But what would the frog have to say about Luffness were it to live in Edinburgh? A gloomy frogly pavane on the window of BBC Queen Street would leave us in no doubt that the golf was off because the rain, snow and mist were on. However, if we were to disagree with

103

the dancing frog and drive towards Longniddry, we would see, as if by miracle, the rain evaporating, the mist clearing, the snow vanishing and Gullane Hill in all its greenness, promising yet another splendid game, stolen against the head.

The official start to winter, add a month or two inland, is the end of October when the clocks allow us a long lie in bed and the rules allow us a short lie on the fairway. The question over what is fairway and what is semi-rough brings forth that sense of fair play instinctive to all members of Luffness. Prolonged impartial arbitration guarantees that all balls are played from where they should be, but most of them after lighting up time.

In the first flush of those Hogmanay resolutions to be sporting, no disputes over preferred lies mar the first competition of the New Year—a foursomes match played with four clubs. The reason is simple. With all error of choice eliminated, players smack the ball with confidence and return scores invariably better than they ever manage throughout the year. However, do our competitors draw the obvious conclusion? No they do not. The guffaws, interruptions and plain inattention that pass for conversation in the clubhouse can be distilled as purely as the gin they consume into one simple sentence—''If I can do that with four clubs what could I have done with fourteen?''

We will leave them there with their gins which they can't account for either, to contemplate that long drawn out saga of the winter foursomes when couples united by handicaps ranging from the suspect to the frankly bogus, join battle for a trophy as ''mythical'' as the Triple Crown.

The game *should* be the thing, but as some sage remarked, ''Winning doesn't matter till you lose''.

Yet no competition can assure the winners of a more speedy slide into oblivion. None gives rise to greater rivalry or to a more fraudulent pretence that we have all entered, specifically to play from whatever hazards our partners have deliberately chosen for us. All the couples but one have to lose, and that pair celebrate their brief triumph with a bottle of club champagne before being more forgotten than those who had nothing to celebrate at all.

Triumphs of another sort—over the desire to sleep a little longer are the hallmark of those other all season foursomes—the dinner matches. These games to be played through the bleakest days of the year seem a great idea when contracted in the warmth of the clubhouse by minds afloat with gin. The contracts are legal and binding and everyone has to honour the promise unless positive proof of infirmity can be produced. To have lost one leg might be accepted, but to be completely legless would not.

And legless indeed was one celebrated member of the dinner fraternity on the night, when he elected to walk ''home'' across the second fairway to the Mallard Hotel in Gullane. Nicknamed at school after one of the more rounded prehistoric monsters, he got as far as the second green before tumbling into a bunker where he lay on his back gasping and motionless. Quite by chance a young couple also in search of a preferred lie, stepped into the bunker baffled by what sounded like the last moments of a feckless bull. Compassion took precedence over love and having helped him to his feet and on his intended way, they proceeded to the extremes of affection in the huge hollow—smoothed out by the Luffness member.

Love is teasing and love is pleasing but when it has teased and pleased, reality does have that nasty habit of doing neither. The earth, cold instead of moving; the young gallant brought to his senses by some remark such as:

"When we are married, promise you won't spend so much time on the golf course," then stupefied again by the grunts of the Luffness member trying to effect an entry into Gullane number three.

By the time he made it, winter had gone, the clocks had moved forward, and the Spring Meeting beckoned members to one of the few medals of the Luffness year. Luffness is not a club for the tyranny of card and pencil. Why all this nonsense about holing out when a gracious concession could have everyone back in the clubhouse toasting the putts they never had to sink.

Nonetheless during this spring weekend, the old rule of not giving any putts we don't fancy ourselves does not apply. Everything has to drop despite the weather which is rather as winter ought to be— flags flattened by a wind straight off the North Pole, rain and the ball, more to the point, having to be played where it lands.

The sportsmanship, natural to club members, is always in evidence and it is not unusual for entrants to withdraw from the Saturday hurricane in the hope that Sunday might be windless. The leading scores then meet each other in trial by combat for the honour of the club championship unless they have already been disqualified by the secretary for conduct unbecoming.

The honoured roll of club champions, inscribed in gold, hang in the dirty bar as an eternal proof of all those who would trade the rigours of the practice ground in favour of strong drink. That they might have some difficulty in actually finding the practice ground is on the cards. Why should they know where it is? A Captain, no less, at an annual general meeting, exasperated by some plaintive proposal for one of those radical changes that threaten a status quo that survived similar threats half a century ago, was heard quite plainly to ask:

"Where is the practice ground?"

For most of the members, practice would just involve grooving in a new flaw which they could well do without by the time the Summer Meeting is upon them. This weekend is without fail the worst of the year; the barometric frog retreating in strict tempo into the Queen Street fridge for warmth; anyone effete enough to hoist a brolly against the rain, hang-gliding even deeper into the rough, and all those putts, short enough to be sunk without praise and short enough to be missed without comment.

But all summer is not a question of missing short putts and a hail storm. Were there no rain, Luffness would not be so green and there are moments in the summer when this greenness is magical. The air heavy with the smell of cut grass, the flag listless, the turf like the road to the Isles, and the long rays from the west touching the trees around Luffness House with a dark mystery. We spend more time musing on our memories than we do making them and to be allowed to repeat them in such idyllic surroundings is a gift from the Gods which preside over Luffness.

The summer rolls on, the weather improves and we mark this rite of passage with yet another medal—the Autumn Meeting where shirt sleeves are not unusual and where, were it not for the calendar, we would think it June. But it is not June and the weather will not reach its full glory until around the end of October when winter begins and the lies are preferred again.

Thomas More who actually preferred the truth though sorely tempted, felt he could not accept membership of Luffness because he would have needed to be a man for all seasons—frequently all on the same day. But the Club did leave its mark. His observations there made him feel the need to create "Utopia"—a haven of order, sobriety and unquestioning submission to the council's will. And another Luffness failing eventually did for him. During his long series with Henry Tudor who was about to go one down with five to play he just lost his head and the king went on to end up six down against no opposition.

Some may not believe this little story but it is our preferred lie.

November 19th, 1974, a water diviner, Mr R. McVitie, was asked to assist in "finding" water.

Because of bad weather the course was officially closed from 21st November to 2nd December 1993.

"NEVER HURRY — REMEMBER TO SMELL THE FLOWERS ALONG THE WAY"
(WALTER HAGEN)

LUFFNESS SUMMER FLORA

by

MARGERY KIMPTON

In common with several other Scottish golf courses, Luffness Links were originally sand dunes, with a flora adapted to coastal conditions. The rough acts as a reservoir for typical dune plants which have successfully combatted the effects of strong drying winds and loose sandy soil (often of high salinity).

Thus, various growth modifications can be seen amongst the plants in the area. Many are low-growing, forming dense tufts or cushions, some with leaves in the form of basal rosettes to reduce water loss. Other leaf features which prevent loss of water by evaporation are leaves with hairs, scales or a reduction of leaves to spines. Many, like the Silverweed, have creeping stems or runners which help to bind the soil.

The areas of scrub are dominated by large clumps of Sea-buckthorn, a thorny shrub easily recognised by its silvery scaly leaves and bright orange berries.

For those interested in identifying plants, all that is necessary is a keen eye, patience (golfers take note!) and a wild flower book—preferably one with illustrations. Some wild flower books group plants according to the flower colour (indicated in plant list). Others group plants according to their family or natural order as exemplified below. Choose a fine day in early summer (a golfer's delight!) and you will find all the plants listed below and many more besides.

Some plants to look for in **sandy areas** are:

Sea pearlwort (white); Wild thyme (purple);
Bird's foot trefoil (yellow); Dove's-foot crane's-bill (pink);
Stork's bill (pink); Tormentil (yellow);
Biting stonecrop (yellow); Silverweed (yellow);
Fieldmouse-ear (white); Heath dog-violet (blue);
Mouse-ear hawkweed (yellow); Yellow trefoil;
Thrift (pink); Common or Heath speedwell
    (lilac)

In the **wetter patches** you will find:

Early marsh orchis (crimson Purple milk vetch;
   purple); Butterwort (purple)—an insect-
Field woodrush (brown);   eating plant with sticky leaves

In the rough **meadowland** farthest from the sea are:

Meadowsweet (white); Cowslip (yellow);
Germander speedwell (blue); Yellow meadow vetchling;
Dyers weed (green); Bush vetch (purple);
Self-heal (purple); Cuckoo flowers (purple)

At the left of the gate at the quarry, is a patch of Shining beauty—a species of Claytonia with small white flowers and fused leaf pairs circling the stem.

One family of flowering plants, easily recognised by the shape of the flower, is the Peaflower family (*Papilionaceae*). Flowers are like those of the garden pea or bean and the plants bear pods as fruits, e.g.:

Purple milk vetch; Bird's foot trefoil;
Yellow trefoil; Yellow meadow vetchling
Bush vetch;

Happy hunting and be heartened by the fact that plants, unlike birds, will at least remain in one place for close examination!

Bibliography
"Collins Pocket Guide to Wild Flowers" (McClintock & Filter).
Keble Martin's "Concise British Flora" (Methuen, now A.B.P.).

The latter is a detailed and very well illustrated book but far from pocket sized.

NATURE CALENDAR

by

ARCHIE MATHIESON

January

When there are falls of snow inland but not on the coast, the clear areas may lead to what are known as "hard weather movements" of birds. Early arrivals are SKYLARKS and several hundred may appear en route for the south. Other birds which follow a similar pattern are the GOLDEN PLOVER, WOODPIGEON and FIELDFARE. GEESE at a distance may be identified by their flying pattern. When they are at a distance they show as Vs or wavy lines. As they fly overhead they are more easy to identify.

GEESE IN FLIGHT

WREN

The buckthorn and other bushes act as a shelter for many species of small bird at night—a roosting place. The WREN, one of the smallest birds, may be there, or near a stone wall. They have a very loud song for such small birds. They feed on a variety of insects.

The SONG THRUSH searches out hibernating SNAILS and takes them to a stone or rock, known as an "anvil". Here they smash the snail until the shell breaks and the snail is devoured—look for the broken shells.

SONG THRUSH

Although the breeding season is still some way away some birds, including PARTRIDGES, are pairing off. Their courtship is a noisy affair with birds calling as they chase rival males. Fights are not uncommon with birds fluttering up to strike with their feet.

PARTRIDGE

FOXES are around but not in great numbers as most of their activity takes place under cover of darkness. Dog foxes will travel many miles in search of a suitable vixen. Their droppings are greyish in colour and contain bones and fur. The tracks may be seen in the bunkers where it is not uncommon for them to bury catches. Note

FOX

the spoor of the fox compared with that of the dog.

The shallow scrapes and droppings of rabbits, particularly at the 9th fairway, are territorial markers. The presence of tufts of rabbit fur indicates that the bucks have been fighting. The buck will sit on one spot for prolonged periods looking after his territory, and a "carpet" of droppings will indicate such spots. Most of the damage done to golf courses takes place during the breeding season. While the main breeding season is the first six months of the year, young may be born as early as Christmas and the New Year.

SPOOR OF FOX

February

"As the days grow longer the cold grows stronger." This is often the coldest month of the year and food supplies are at their lowest for birds and animals alike. Flocks of seed-eating birds move around the countryside in search of food. One of these is the GOLDFINCH. A colourful little bird with red, white and black on the head and the broad bands of yellow on the wings which help to identify it. This is one of the birds which used to be trapped and sold to live in misery in a cage.

The MERLIN is a falcon which may be seen along the coast in winter. The male is not much larger than a mistle thrush and as with many birds of prey the female is larger than the male. When hunting it flies low and fast before rising above its victim and striking. Because of its small size most of its prey are small birds such as skylarks, meadow pippet, etc.

Winter may bring the HOODED CROW, usually a single bird; it is easily identified by its grey "waistcoat".

Hares were once very common, but their numbers have diminished considerably and there is no sign that this has been reversed, nor is the reason for this decline known. The behaviour during the breeding season has earned it the name of the "mad March hare". The "boxing" can start as early as January.

SPOOR OF DOG

GOLDFINCH

MERLIN

HOODED CROW

When they were common it was not unusual to see ten or more hares involved in this behaviour. The young hare is known as a LEVERET. The doe leaves them singly in separate locations and returns to suckle them. This helps with their survival as predators will only find one of the brood.

STOATS catch rabbits, and a variety of birds (including eggs and young). Most of these which we encounter are likely to have retained some of their brown fur on their heads. The white coat is only of use to them if we have snow, without which they are more easily seen. Part of the tail always remains black.

HARE

March

With the increase of daylight many birds can be heard singing, and among these is the SKYLARK. It is the male that we frequenltly see and hear soaring high over its territory and moving vertically as he does so. The rough is an ideal place for skylarks to nest.

STOAT (ERMINE)

I came to East Lothian in 1970 and had been here for six years before I recorded my first MAGPIE. They are on the increase and nest locally. The nest is a large domed affair with an entrance hole on one side, and is built with small sticks. The pied plumage, long tail and constant chattering make them easy to identify.

MAGPIE

The LAPWING, better known in Scotland as the PEEWIT, is one of the birds to watch for. The display flight is quite spectacular with the birds climbing and tumbling down as if they were out of control. They fly from the nest and have a distress call to direct attention away from the area. In the winter they gather in large flocks and flight to and from the shore.

LAPWING

The SHORT-EARED OWL hunts by day and may be seen, sometimes in pairs, as they circle overhead. They return to Scandinavia to breed.

A large grey bird with long trailing legs and a black and white head drawn into the neck can only be a HERON. Aberlady Bay is a

SHORTEARED OWL

111

good place to see them. They feed on toads and frogs which are just coming out of hibernation.

One of the first migrants to appear just before the end of the month is the WHEATEAR. The count is over 100 birds. The males are the first to turn up and they have grey and black plumage with buff on the breast, while the rump is white.

WHEATEAR (Male)

The ROE DEER which are quite common on and around the area may suddenly break cover. The buck's antlers may still be covered with a furry material known as "VELVET". This protects the antlers when they are still growing. Later the deer will rub its antlers against young trees to remove the velvet.

We can expect to see HEDGEHOGS appearing out of hibernation. Normally they come out in the late evening and hunt for food at night, but at this time they are sometimes seen during the day.

ROE DEER with 'velvet'.

TOADS will also be coming out of hibernation, and may cross the course making for the ponds on Aberlady Bay. I have counted more than 20 on the road to the sewage works. Toads have a dry, pimply skin and move by very short jumps or by crawling. The frog has a moist, shining bright-coloured skin and moves by leaping.

TOAD

If you come on a large hairy caterpillar at this time it is that of the FOX MOTH. They, too, hibernate over winter and emerge in spring then make a cocoon in the ground and later the moth will appear.

April

One of the most eagerly awaited spring migrants is the SWALLOW.

SWALLOW

On bushes around the golf course look for the tiny WILLOW WARBLER and consider that it has flown all the way from Africa. They have a greenish olive-brown plumage and an attractive sweet song on a descending scale.

The MEADOW PIPPIT may be seen throughout the year, and some nest in the rough. Many are winter visitors from

WILLOW WARBLER

Scandinavia and Russia. From the middle of the month flocks of these birds may be seen leaving for their breeding areas. They circle to a fair height, then fly out east or north-east calling all the time.

SHELDUCK

Some of the PINK-FOOTED GEESE and GREYLAG GEESE will still be leaving, flying high, almost out of sight and heading over the Forth.

The large MISTLE THRUSH, with a beak full of worms, may still be feeding young in the nest.

In most ducks the male is more colourful than the female, as the latter has to remain inconspicuous as she cares for her young. One of the exceptions is the SHELLDUCK where the male and female are similar. She has no need to have a dull plumage as she makes her nest in a rabbit burrow. Keep a look out for pairs prospecting for a suitable site. The noisy REDSHANK may be around as it performs its circular display. I have found nests on the edge of the course and on nearby fields.

REDSHANK
Display flight

The MOLE is a most unwelcome visitor to any golf course. The "mole hills" must be a greenkeeper's nightmare. The male is a black mammal, but during the past twenty years I have heard of two fawn-coloured specimens trapped on Luffness New Golf Course.

MOLE

May

Large numbers of EIDER DUCK may be seen on the fairways at this time, mainly in the morning. The black and white males and brown females are easily identified and are "quite" tame. Many of their eggs are taken by CROWS and gulls. Look for the "sucked" eggs which are a dirty olive colour. PHEASANT and PARTRIDGE eggs are also liable to be damaged by scavengers.

EIDER DUCK (Male)

One of the birds of prey which hunt regularly over the course is the KESTREL. This bird is recognised by its habit of hovering above its selected hunting area. It feeds on VOLES, MICE, small birds and insects.

KESTREL

Bird migration reaches a peak about this time and among those to look for are the CUCKOO, SWIFT, SWALLOW and HOUSE MARTIN. Large numbers of swallows and house martins in particular may be seen moving through.

The SMALL HEATH BUTTERFLY is worth looking for on the course. The upper surface of the wings is pale tawny with a black spot near the tip of each forewing. When it closes its wings the underside of the forewing is pale orange. The earlier caterpillars feed on grass.

The insect most prevalent, and seen in huge numbers, is the large ST MARK'S FLY. Dense clouds of them may be seen flying, often around the bushes. Recognised by their long hanging legs they play an important role in pollinating the flowers of HAWTHORN and other bushes. They are a welcome source of food for many of our birds.

SWIFT

HOUSE MARTIN

June

Look for the OYSTERCATCHERS flying over on their way to the coast. Many of them nest on farm land, and it is common to see single birds. Male and female share the duties of incubating the eggs and the "off duty" bird returns to the coast to feed. This is one of the few waders which will carry food to its young and so it is not uncommon to see a bird with a MUSSEL or SAND EEL in its mouth.

If you see a skein of geese at this time they are likely to be CANADA GEESE. They are on their way to the Beauly Firth where birds of various species gather to moult.

From time to time the SHORT TAILED VOLE numbers reach plague proportions, and the rough can harbour large numbers of these small mammals. They have a network of runs through the grass and build a ball-shaped nest for their young. They are a ready source of food for KESTREL, SHORT-EARED OWL, STOAT, WEASEL and FOX. I have watched stoats and weasels on the course, the former frequently playing with moths

SMALL HEATH BUTTERFLY

OYSTERCATCHER

WEASEL

near the 15th tee, the latter scurrying across the fairways looking for prey. On occasion they catch quite large rabbits.

The only blue butterfly you can hope to see is the COMMON BLUE BUTTERFLY.

On the stalks of rough grass you may find the cocoon made by the caterpillar of the SIX SPOT BURNET MOTH. It is pale yellow in colour.

GRASSHOPPERS are around now, but with the arrival of the frost in the autumn, they all die. The species persists because the eggs are deposited at the roots of the grass. MILLIPEDES, many of them dead, are found in the bunkers. During the dry weather it would appear that they cannot get out of the sand, and are dehydrated by the sun.

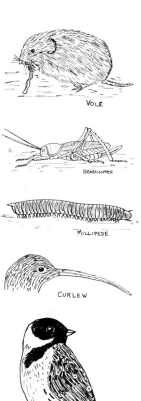

VOLE

GRASSHOPPER

MILLIPEDE

CURLEW

July

Increasing numbers of CURLEW will be seen flying over the course as they fly to and from the coast. They feed in the fields.

The REED BUNTING nests on the course and is recognised by his black head and throat, and white collar. He has an attractive song as he sings from the top of a bush or tall plant.

Keep a lookout for ROE DEER, not uncommonly crossing the fairways en route to the sewage area. They usually produce twins, so you may be fortunate enough to see does with their young.

The SHREW is one of the smallest of our mammals. It feeds on EARTHWORMS, INSECTS, etc. They have a squeaky call but it is so high pitched that many people are unable to hear it. The males fight with each other, sometimes to the death, and so you may find a dead one.

The RABBIT population is usually at its peak now. Since the 1950s rabbits have been infected with the myxomatosis virus. When it first appeared it almost decimated the rabbit population, but with the passage of time some appear to have developed an immunity to the virus and the numbers are rising again.

The red and black SIX SPOTTED BURNET

REED BUNTING
(Male)

MEADOW BROWN BUTTERFLY

SHREW

MOTH appears this month and may appear in profusion. It takes its name from the three pairs of red spots on each wing. When these are closed the two spots nearest the head merge into one.

6 SPOT BURNET MOTH

The caterpillar of the FOX MOTH is velvety with fine gold rings. As it grows in size it changes colour and develops into the hairy caterpillar which we associate with our greens and fairways.

The DARK-LIPPED HEDGE SNAIL is common on the course. Some are yellow, others fawn and many with dark bands around the shell. All have a black lip to the shell. During dry spells they "lie up" to conserve moisture. The rain brings them out in profusion.

DARK LIPPED HEDGE SNAIL

August

The three crows common in the area are the CARRION CROW, ROOK and JACKDAW. The carrion crow has a deep croaking call. The rook has a bare face and a higher pitched call than the carrion crow. The jackdaw is the smallest of the three with a grey nape and a pale eye. The MAGPIE is also a member of the crow family.

CARRION CROW

Flocks of STARLINGS, sometimes in large numbers, often feed on the fairways. They probe into the ground and it is suspected that they are searching for wireworms.

Look for the WHEATEARS returning south. They spend the winter in Africa.

Foxes often catch more food than they can eat. They will bury a rabbit or a bird and return for it later. I have known them to use a bunker for this purpose.

ROOK

The CATERPILLAR of the WHITE ERMINE MOTH is one of the most common of the hairy caterpillars. They are brown with a red-orange stripe along the back. They move faster than most of the other caterpillars.

BUMBLE-BEES are usually abundant at this time. Most that you see will be the small worker-bees. They collect pollen and nectar to feed the bee grubs, thus allowing the

JACKDAW

116

queen bee to devote her time to egg-laying. You may be surprised to know that in Britain we have around 240 different kinds of bees.

The GRASSHOPPER produces its "song" by rubbing its hind legs against its wings. A row of tiny pegs on the leg strike a wing vein producing vibrations which we hear as a chirp.

BLACK SLUG

The large BLACK SLUG, like the snail, lays down a mucous pathway along which it can glide.

September

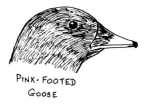

PINK-FOOTED GOOSE

Two questions that are frequently asked this month are "Have you seen the geese yet?" or "Are the geese here yet?" The geese in question are the PINK-FOOTED GEESE which arrive from Iceland to spend the winter with us. They usually get here around the middle of the month. There can be few more impressive sights than skeins of geese passing overhead, and their distinctive wild calls.

By the end of the month the REDWINGS should have arrived from Scandinavia. These thrush-like birds take their name from the red patch on the flank and under the wings.

REDWING

Throughout the winter SHORT-EARED OWLS hunt for their prey over the course. Many that arrive in the area are believed to be migrants, like the redwings, from Scandinavia. They roost on the ground.

This is the time for many of our small birds to gather into flocks and they may be seen on fields adjacent to the course.

SHORTEARED OWL

TOADS will be on the move again as they prepare for hibernation for the winter.

WASPS can be particularly common at this time and are liable to be very aggressive. In Britain we have more than 290 different species of wasp, but only a few are "stinging" wasps.

Another insect that we have in this area is the MOSQUITO. They pierce our skin to suck blood—only the females do this. In those who are sensitive, such a bite can cause considerable local reaction necessitating medical care.

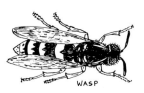

WASP

117

The FOX MOTH CATERPILLAR will be fully developed by now. They are the large hairy caterpillars, chestnut brown with black markings, which are often on the greens and fairways. Handle them at your peril! They give off a secretion which can cause a skin irritation. I have known of children requiring medical care after handling these caterpillars.

CATERPILLAR OF FOX MOTH

WHOOPER SWAN (Head)

FIELDFARE

ROBIN

GREAT TIT

BLUE TIT

October

The largest of the northern migrants which we will see is the WHOOPER SWAN. They nest in Iceland, northern Europe and northern Asia. They fly to and from the coast to the inland fields where they feed. Their flight line takes them over the course. The loud "whoop-a-hoop" flight call will alert us to their presence.

If you see a single, noisy PINK-FOOTED GEESE flying over, it is likely that it has become separated from its family. It will fly around trying to contact its family, as geese are capable of recognising each other's call.

Most years large numbers of FIELDFARES are present in the adjoining fields. Many are migrants and spend the winter here. They are large members of the thrush family with harsh, chattering calls. Look for them feeding on the orange berries of the SEA BUCKTHORN.

STARLINGS crossing the North Sea to spend the winter here may collect in large numbers. Flocks, particularly in the failing light, pass through flying west or south-west.

The ROBIN is probably our best known bird and can often be seen around the course. They are not shy, and sing throughout the winter. They have a persistent "tick-tick" call.

In your garden you will be able to welcome the GREAT TIT and the BLUE TIT. They are frequent visitors to our bird tables. They are not uncommon on the golf course in the bushes, where they feed. The great tit is the largest of the family with a black head and white cheeks and black down the breast. The blue tit, like the other tits, is a very acrobatic bird. Mainly blue, it has a yellow-green colour on its back and yellow underneath. Flocks of LONG-TAILED TITS, though less common, may be seen from time to time.

LONG-TAILED TIT

November

If you disturb a WOODCOCK from the rough at this time it is likely to be a migrant resting after crossing from the North Sea. Country folklore tells us that the November full moon is the ''Woodcock Moon'' as it is claimed that many of these birds take advantage of the moon to migrate.

WOODCOCK

The BLACKBIRD is a common bird with the male black in colour with an orange-yellow bill and a yellow ring around the eye. The females are brown with dark markings on the breast.

BLACKBIRD (Male)

There are large flocks of CHAFFINCHES on stubble fields adjacent to the course. They nest on bushes in the rough. The male has a slate-blue head, chestnut back and pink-brown underparts. There are white patches and bars on the wings and white edges to the tail. The female is yellow-brown in colour with the same markings as the male.

The large HERRING GULL has a silver-grey back and pink legs. The bill is yellow with a red spot near the tip of the lower jaw. In the winter the head is flecked with brown. You will see them on the fairways performing their ''foot stamping'' routine. In this they stand on one foot and pat the ground with the other, or use both feet alternately. The object is to bring the EARTHWORMS to the surface. It appears that the worms mistake the stamping for heavy rain and come up rather than risk drowning in their burrows.

CHAFFINCH (Male)

The SHORT-EARED OWL deposits pellets which are in fact regurgitated material. Your young children or grandchildren will be able to place these in warm water and then tease them open with two large needles to release the contents of these grey pellets which not infrequently contain remnants of the skull and lower jaw of a vole. They kill their prey

HERRING GULL

OWL PELLETS

119

by striking from behind the head, and this can be confirmed.

SPARROWHAWK

December

The SPARROWHAWK has increased in numbers in the last decade. It has a blunt head, broad wings and a fairly long tail. They catch small birds, but the female, which is considerably larger than the male, is capable of killing birds as large as a WOODPIGEON. Considering the number of birds caught by hawks and falcons it is surprising how seldom we see it happen. Frequently all we may find is a scattering of feathers where the bird has been caught and devoured. This usually takes place in the shelter of a bush or other cover. You may find legs, bill and feathers that are all that remain after the bird has been eaten.

With the short winter days many birds have to spend most of the daylight hours searching for food. Male and female ROBINS have a winter territory of their own which they defend against other robins.

COCK PHEASANT

The PHEASANT is a common bird on the golf course and their call can frequently be heard behind the 3rd fairway where they roost.

SEA BUCKTHORN

The orange berries of the SEA BUCKTHORN provide a source of food for many of our birds including BLACKBIRD, FIELDFARE and REDWING. Some 75 CARRION CROWS have been seen eating the berries on the clump of blackthorn at the sewage works. If you have any reason to have a brush with blackthorn you will be aware that it is armed with very sharp, strong thorns.

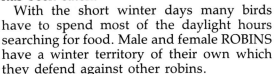

REDWING

We usually associate insects with the warmer weather, but there is one insect which can be seen throughout the winter. The slightest blink of sun will tempt the WINTER GNAT. They appear as a "column" of insects rising and falling in quick succession in the shelter of the bushes.

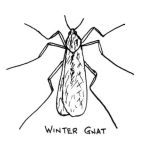

WINTER GNAT

And as the sun sets in the west, all is still. We remember and thank those who have sought to foster and enrich the spirit of our Club.

"The past is a story told—
The future may be writ in gold."

Anon.

APPENDICES

THE LECONFIELD GOLD MEDAL PRESENTED IN 1895 BY LORD LECONFIELD FOR THE BEST SCRATCH SCORE AT THE SPRING MEETING

		Strokes
1895	F. G. Tait	76
1896	T. T. Gray	81
1897	F. G. Tait	78
1898	A. W. Robertson	80
1899	A. W. Robertson	77
1900	A. W. Robertson Durham	86
1901	A. W. Robertson Durham	84
1902	J. E. Gordon	79
1903	A. W. Robertson Durham	80
1904	A. G. Tait	81
1905	D. Currie.	77
1906	D. Currie.	75
1907	G. W. Walker.	76
1908	J. Monro Hunter	79
1909	A. W. Robertson Durham	81
1910	Douglas Currie	87
1911	J. A. Robertson Durham	80
1912	A. W. Robertson Durham	75
1913	J. A. Robertson Durham	78
1914	Douglas Currie •	74
1915-18	First World War Period	..
1919	J. C. Rose	85
1920	P. C. Smythe.	78
1921	W. C. White	77
1922	W. B. Torrance	73
1923	A. Burn Murdoch	72
1924	W. B. Torrance	67
1925	Dr A. Cleland.	73
1926	D. S. Weir	74
1927	W. C. White	77
1928	R. Gordon Henderson	75
1929	W. B. Torrance	76
1930	Dr A. Cleland.	77
1931	W. B. Torrance	74
1932	W. C. White	77
1933	D. M. Stocks	71
1934	Dr A. Cleland.	73
1935	W. C. White	74
1936	A. G. Thornton	74
1937	James Milne	73

1938	W. A. Cochrane	73
1939	W. B. Torrance	76
1940-45	Second World War Period	..
1946	R. Wight	77
1947	J. S. Robertson	78
1948	J. H. Lamb	72
1949	E. N. MacMeeken	72
1950	R. Wight	73
1951	J. Leckie	74
1952	J. Sands	70
1953	J. Leckie	73
1954	J. Sands	73
1955	J. Leckie	70
1956	W. D. Mayer	72
1957	Dr A. G. Donald	73
1958	R. Wright	73
1959	A. W. Small	68
1960	R. F. Galloway	71
1961	J. McNee	72
1962	J. A. Lang	72
1963	W. B. M. Laird	75
1964	A. W. Small	71
1965	J. Leckie	72
1966	A. Forrest	72
1967	W. B. M. Laird	71
1968	W. B. M. Laird	72
1969	A. J. Low	69
1970	{ A. J. D. Blaikie { Dr D. R. Sandison.	} 74
1971	Dr A. G. Donald	76
1972	K. W. Paterson-Brown	73
1973	Dr A. G. Donald	71
1974	I. M. Paterson	71
1975	J. R. Inglis	72
1976	J. M. Croall	74
1977	J. R. Inglis	74
1978	I. D. Miller	72
1979	I. D. Miller	77
1980	J. R. Inglis	68
1981	{ J. R. Inglis { M. S. J. McEwan	} 76
1982	J. R. Inglis	74
1983	R. T. Hamilton	73
1984	M. C. Leslie	73
1985	Dr A. G. Leitch	76
1986	M. S. J. McEwan	72

		Strokes
1987	L. D. Mitchell.	74
1988	C. Cuthbert	73
1989	C. Cuthbert	67
1990	C. Cuthbert	73
1991	{ C. Cuthbert . . . . }	70
	{ R. M. Gaunt . . . . }	
1992	A. R. Corbett	74
1993	I. Smith	74

THE ROSS MEDAL PRESENTED IN 1895 BY
A. M. ROSS FOR THE BEST HANDICAP SCORE AT THE
AUTUMN MEETING

		Strokes Net
1895	W. T. Armour	85
1896	J. M. Bow	80
1897	George Chiene	83
1898	J. D. Paterson.	82
1899	James Reid	82
1900	E. R. Turnbull	82
1901	Ian Macintyre	79
1902	Hon. Evan Charteris	77
1903	W. T. Armour	75
1904	J. I. Gillespie .	81
1905	A. S. Drybrough	73
1906	J. T. Bywater .	75
1907	J. W. Struthers	70
1908	D. C. Greenlees	73
1909	W. J. Guild	78
1910	J. A. Robertson Durham	74
1911	J. A. Robertson Durham	73
1912	H. D. Lawrie .	76
1913	A. G. Cairns .	75
1914-18	First World War Period	..
1919	E. Fearenside .	83
1920	K. Sanderson .	72
1921	H. Philipson .	77
1922	A. Burn Murdoch .	72
1923	G. W. Shearer	75
1924	D. M. Stocks .	70
1925	W. B. Torrance	75
1926	R. Gordon Henderson .	73
1927	R. Whitelaw, Jr.	71
1928	D. R. Mackenzie	70
1929	D. M. Stocks .	76
1930	J. A. W. Beaton	73
1931	W. F. G. Normand	63
1932	Dr W. R. Martine .	67
1933	G. K. Maclennan .	66
1934	C. J. Nicolson.	65
1935	A. Prentice	69
1936	J. Irvine Carswell .	67
1937	W. W. Duncan	67
1938	George Walker	67
1939-45	Second World War Period .	..

Year	Name	Strokes Net
1946	J. Flockhart	68
1947	Dr Wm. McLean	69
1948	James Milne	67
1949	A. J. Dobbie	65
1950	C. Lambert, Jr.	68
1951	H. Rogers	67
1952	J. Stewart	64
1953	A. C. R. Annan	67
1954	G. L. Stewart	64
1955	J. R. Scott	65
1956	G. G. Thomson	71
1957	J. H. McNicol	63
1958	J. McNee	66
1959	Lt.-Col. R. A. Buchanan-Dunlop . . .	66
1960	J. C. Wilson	69
1961	J. C. Wilson	69
1962	W. J. Kinloch Anderson	64
1963	F. D. Burnett	69
1964	D. S. Berrie	65
1965	J. B. Anderstrem	67
1966	D. M. Smith	65
1967	C. T. Rankin	68
1968	I. Maclean	69
1969	A. C. Munro	66
1970	R. G. H. Smith	63
1971	{ Dr G. H. Mathieson . . . . . } { J. Brown . . . . }	67
1972	N. W. Ramage	64
1973	Dr W. D. MacLennan	66
1974	{ I. M. Paterson . . . . . . } { P. F. Bruce . . . . }	65
1975	J. W. Oswald	66
1976	J. J. Carmichael	65
1977	Dr G. H. Mathieson	63
1978	D. L. Millar	63
1979	A. Douglas	62
1980	D. A. Ferguson	64
1981	W. F. Noble	65
1982	{ A. G. Scott . . . . } { R. M. MacArthur . . . . . . }	66
1983	D. M. Hall	61
1984	J. Nimmo	61
1985	P. M. Blyth	71
1986	F. Guy	68
1987	Lt.-Col. W. H. Chapman	66

		Strokes Net
1988	P. J. Waddell	63
1989	A. R. Corbett	65
1990	T. A. M. Myles	63
1991	J. I. Dunlop	69
1992	{ J. G. Simpson . . . . } { W. W. Park . . . . }	63
1993	{ C. E. S. Cairns . . . . } { G. M. McLachlan . . . . }	65

THE HOPE MEDAL PRESENTED IN 1895 BY
HENRY WALTER HOPE FOR THE BEST SCRATCH SCORE AT THE AUTUMN MEETING

		Strokes
1895	F. G. Tait	86
1896	Major D. A. Kinloch	82
1897	A. M. Ross	86
1898	F. G. Tait	79
1899	David Lyell	88
1900	A. M. Ross	88
1901	W. T. Armour	83
1902	Angus Macdonald	80
1903	W. T. Armour	77
1994	Col. D. A. Kinloch	81
1905	A. W. Robertson Durham	74
1906	J. Monro Hunter	79
1907	J. W. Struthers	75
1908	G. W. Walker	77
1909	W. J. Guild	80
1910	J. A. Robertson Durham	74
1911	J. A. Robertson Durham	71
1912	A. W. Robertson Durham	78
1913	A. W. Robertson Durham	77
1914-18	First World War Period	..
1919	J. A. Robertson Durham	82
1920	W. B. Torrance	73
1921	G. C. Manford	75
1922	A. Burn Murdoch	72
1923	W. B. Torrance	76
1924	W. B. Torrance	71
1925	W. B. Torrance	72
1926	J. C. Rose	74
1927	R. Gordon Henderson	75
1928	A. G. Thornton	73
1929	Herbert Millar	79
1930	J. Stanley Graham	75
1931	W. B. Torrance	71
1932	W. B. Torrance / W. A. Cochrane	71
1933	W. C. White	73
1934	Dr A. Cleland	71
1935	W. B. Torrance	69
1936	W. A. Cochrane	72
1937	D. S. Weir	74
1938	James Milne / W. B. Torrance	73

1939-45	Second World War Period	..
1946	A. J. D. Blaikie	72
1947	T. C. Scott	75
1948	James Milne	68
1949	James Milne	70
1950	T. C. Scott	74
1951	J. Sands	73
1952	J. Milne	70
1953	T. C. Scott	71
1954	G. L. Stewart	71
1955	A. W. Small	69
1956	Dr J. L. Cowan	77
1957	J. Leckie	74
1958	J. A. Lang	72
1959	J. A. Lang	73
1960	A. C. Gardiner	76
1961	J. McNee	71
1962	W. A. Whitelaw	70
1963	G. B. Hendry	76
1964	C. T. Rankin	73
1965	J. McNee	74
1966	H. V. Stone	72
1967	C. T. Rankin	72
1968	{ H. V. Stone . . . . { T. Gray . . . . }	74
1969	{ A. J. Low . . . . { L. D. Mitchell . . . . }	74
1970	{ C. T. Rankin . . . . { T. Gray . . . . }	71
1971	R. R. Jack	74
1972	H. F. Neilson	74
1973	{ J. R. Inglis . . . . { J. O. R. Martin . . . . }	75
1974	I. M. Paterson	68
1975	{ M. C. Leslie . . . . { A. D. Macintyre . . . . }	76
1976	R. R. Jack	68
1977	M. R. Dewar	72
1978	A. F. Dawson	77
1979	J. R. Inglis	72
1980	J. R. Inglis	69
1981	J. R. Inglis	74
1982	M. S. J. McEwan	71
1983	{ R. T. Hamilton . . . . { J. R. Inglis . . . . }	72
1984	J. R. Inglis	69

Year	Name		Strokes
1985	J. D. D. Elvin		80
1986	C. Cuthbert		76
1987	C. Cuthbert		70
1988	P. J. Waddell		73
1989	A. R. Corbett		72
1990	{ C. Cuthbert . . . . }		72
	{ I. Smith . . . . }		
1991	A. S. Mayer		75
1992	D. P. Allan		70
1993	I. Smith		70

THE SILVER QUAICH PRESENTED IN 1895 BY
JAMES REID AND W. T. ARMOUR FOR THE BEST HANDICAP
SCORE AT THE SPRING MEETING

		Strokes Net
1895	F. G. Tait	80
1896	T. T. Gray	81
1897	H. D. Lawrie	82
1898	A. W. Robertson	80
1899	A. W. Robertson	77
1900	W. T. Armour	84
1901	L. G. Thomas	84
1902	J. E. Gordon	79
1903	Ian Macintyre	78
1904	W. Ritchie	78
1905	D. A. Guild	71
1906	W. J. Guild	75
1907	G. W. Walker	76
1908	John Moir	73
1909	L. Wood Smith	76
1910	R. G. Bowie	81
1911	Jas. Galloway	78
1912	H. L. Fleming	77
1913	W. Purves	74
1914	A. Druitt	74
1915-18	First World War Period	..
1919	A. J. Lawrie	84
1920	P. C. Smythe	78
1921	F. L. M. Tod	74
1922	{ W. B. Torrance { J. M. Cooper	} 76
1923	C. O. Ainslie	69
1924	W. B. Torrance	70
1925	Dr A. Cleland	74
1926	D. S. Weir	72
1927	G. H. Normand	74
1928	Herbert Millar	73
1929	Prof. John Fraser	70
1930	John Cruickshank, Jr.	73
1931	R. N. Fairgrieve	73
1932	Hector Laing	71
1933	G. R. Lawson	67
1934	Fred. Mills	71
1935	Dr R. C. Scott Dow	66
1936	D. M. Boyd	68
1937	Sir Wm. J. Thomson	68

Year	Name	Strokes Net
1938	Stanley Bennet	67
1939	J. B. Matheson	68
1940-45	Second World War Period	..
1946	R. Wight	77
1947	J. S. Robertson	74
1948	J. H. Lamb	69
1949	A. Smith	67
1950	J. Brown	71
1951	E. R. L. Walker	67
1952	W. Carnie	63
1953	F. R. Maguire	66
1954	D. S. Dougal	66
1955	J. Leckie	66
1956	Dr F. C. Laing	65
1957	H. Smart	66
1958	J. D. W. Spence	67
1959	C. Lambert	63
1960	J. J. Millar	65
1961	J. B. Taylor	64
1962	J. S. Deane	65
1963	R. W. Gardiner	66
1964	F. D. Burnet	66
1965	G. R. Harland	66
1966	Dr F. C. Laing	64
1967	W. O. Maguire	65
1968	J. Brown / I. Maclean / J. S. C. Williamson	66
1969	R. G. Graham	63
1970	A. J. D. Blaikie / W. Bell	68
1971	Dr A. G. Donald	69
1972	E. B. Robertson	64
1973	Dr W. A. Simpson / A. H. White	66
1974	R. B. M. Graham	62
1975	F. C. B. Black	66
1976	A. M. Drummond	66
1977	L. A. Thain	66
1978	G. K. Thomson / M. Warrack	64
1979	D. A. Ferguson / A. H. Lamont / I. P. MacIntosh	69

133

		Strokes Net
1980	{ J. R. Inglis { J. H. A. Mackenzie { J. J. Carmichael	66
1981	W. D. Henderson .	66
1982	C. S. G. Wallace .	64
1983	J. S. Liddle	63
1984	W. G. Carnie	60
1985	M. R. Dewar .	64
1986	Dr D. Bain	62
1987	K. G. Hart	63
1988	W. M. Henry .	66
1989	H. Nobbs	65
1990	D. C. R. Graham .	65
1991	{ J. D. L. Fairbairn { J. A. Black	64
1992	A. W. Skinner	65
1993	J. M. Kyle	63

THE TRAYNER CUP FIRST PRESENTED IN 1896 BY
LORD TRAYNER FOR THE BEST SCRATCH SCORE AT THE
SUMMER MEETING

		Strokes
1949	J. Milne	76
1950	W. J. Maguire	74
1951	T. C. Scott	73
1952	C. H. Johnston	73
1953	A. W. Small	71
1954	R. Wright	71
1955	G. B. Hendry	70
1956	J. Sands	72
1957	A. J. D. Blaikie	71
1958	D. S. Dougal	70
1959	A. F. Simpson	71
1960	J. A. Simpson	71
1961	D. S. Dougal	71
1962	D. R. J. Stewart	72
1963	W. B. M. Laird	70
1964	C. T. Rankin	71
1965	A. Forrest	71
1966	T. Gray	70
1967	W. B. M. Laird	69
1968	D. M. Greenhough	69
1969	{ W. B. M. Laird { S. Macrae, Jr.	74
1970	{ T. Gray { A. J. D. Blaikie	72
1971	A. J. Low	72
1972	E. B. Robertson	72
1973	R. E. Simpson	71
1974	R. R. Jack	72
1975	M. R. Dewar	72
1976	J. M. Croall	69
1977	W. D. Henderson	73
1978	L. W. McConachie	73
1979	J. R. Inglis	73
1980	M. S. J. McEwan	72
1981	{ J. R. Inglis { L. D. Mitchell	72
1982	I. M. Paterson	72
1983	I. M. Paterson	67
1984	F. Davidson	71
1985	J. R. Inglis	74
1986	C. Cuthbert	68
1987	C. Cuthbert	73

		Strokes
1988	C. L. Wood	68
1989	J. R. Inglis	70
1990	T. M. Lamb	71
1991	J. R. Inglis	68
1992	R. M. Gaunt	70
1993	{ J. D. D. Elvin . . . . { D. P. Allan . . . . }	74

THE BLOXSOM TROPHY PRESENTED IN 1900 BY
W. G. BLOXSOM FOR THE BEST HANDICAP SCORE AT TWO
OUT OF THREE MEETINGS

		Strokes Net
1900	W. T. Armour	166
1901	W. T. Armour	167
1902	J. I. Gillespie	160
1903	W. T. Armour	160
1904	J. I. Gillespie	168
1905	D. A. Guild	153
1906	W. J. Guild	152
1907	W. J. Guild	158
1908	Allan Rae	159
1909	Allan Rae	158
1910	R. G. Bowie	163
1911	J. A. Robertson Durham	155
1912	H. L. Fleming	156
1913	J. T. B. Bywater	154
1914-18	First World War Period	..
1919	J. T. B. Bywater	174
1920	P. C. Smythe	154
1921	G. C. Manford	160
1922	A. Burn Murdoch	154
1923	C. O. Ainslie	152
1924	W. B. Torrance	144
1925	J. A. W. Beaton	151
1926	D. S. Weir	153
1927	J. A. W. Beaton	153
1928	A. G. Thornton	149
1929	D. M. Stocks	153
1930	J. A. W. Beaton	150
1931	W. F. G. Normand	139
1932	A. Ernest Miller	147
1933	G. R. Lawson	139
1934	E. B. Robertson	143
1935	A. D. Wood	140
1936	J. Irvine Carswell	143
1937	C. J. Nicolson	140
1938	Dr Wm. McLean	145
1939-45	Second World War Period	..
1946	{ W. J. Maguire { Jack Sands	} 151
1947	Dr Wm. McLean	147
1948	G. L. Stewart	145
1949	A. J. Dobbie	139

1950	Dr M. C. K. Finlayson	140
1951	{ V. A. Wood Hawks . . . . . . } H. Rogers	} 137
1952	J. Stewart	133
1953	D. S. Dougal.	136
1954	G. L. Stewart	133
1955	E. N. Macmeeken	135
1956	S. Macrae	130
1957	{ C. R. Sanderson . . . . . . } Dr T. S. Torrance	} 130
1958	J. McNee	131
1959	{ Dr M. C. K. Finlayson . . . . . } A. W. Small	} 135
1960	{ J. J. Millar . . . . } E. G. M. More	} 134
1961	C. D. A. Cousland	132
1962	{ E. W. Brown . . . . . . } F. D. Burnet	} 134
1963	R. W. Gardiner	135
1964	F. D. Burnet	134
1965	{ R. B. Gilroy . . . . . . } K. W. Paterson-Brown	} 136
1966	{ K. S. Holmes . . . . . . } R. I. Marshall	} 136
1967	W. B. M. Laird	133
1968	R. Aitken	134
1969	M. R. Dewar.	133
1970	A. J. Dobbie	130
1971	J. H. A. McKenzie	136
1972	E. B. Robertson	128
1973	Dr W. A. Simpson	134
1974	R. B. M. Graham.	129
1975	A. D. Macintyre	131
1976	M. J. Bell	130
1977	M. S. Mayer	133
1978	D. L. Millar	131
1979	A. Douglas	134
1980	D. A. Ferguson	131
1981	J. M. Cassells	131
1982	R. M. MacArthur.	134
1983	D. M. Hall	129
1984	P. C. Shanks	130
1985	M. R. Dewar.	138
1987	J. J. Degnan	131
1988	{ D. J. S. Crichton . . . . . . } M. B. Livingston	} 134

		Strokes Net
1989	{ J. R. Inglis . . . . } { M. Walls . . . . }	134
1990	{ T. A. M. Myles . . . . } { C. E. Paterson . . . . }	133
1991	Dr G. Kennedy	131
1992	D. J. Kirkpatrick	133
1993	J. M. Kyle	135

THE TAIT SILVER MEDAL PRESENTED IN 1901 BY
A. G. TAIT FOR THE SECOND BEST SCRATCH SCORE AT THE SPRING MEETING

		Strokes
1901	J. L. Gillespie.	86
1902	A. G. Tait	79
1903	Angus McDonald .	83
1904	Dr L. R. Gray.	84
1905	A. W. Robertson Durham	79
1906	A. W. Robertson Durham	78
1907	D. Currie.	77
1908	Ian Macintyre.	81
1909	D. A. Guild	82
1910	H. J. Ross	90
1911	H. J. Ross	81
1912	H. L. Fleming.	81
1913	J. T. B. Bywater	79
1914	J. A. Robertson Durham	76
1915-19	First World War Period	..
1920	G. C. Manford	79
1921	D. Currie.	77
1922	F. L. M. Tod	76
1923	A. M. McDonald	72
1924	W. C. White	72
1925	J. A. Robertson Durham	76
1926	A. M. McDonald	75
1927	Jas. Milne	78
1928	{ W. B. Torrance { Herbert Millar	} 76
1929	{ J. S. Graham . { R. G. Henderson . { Dr A. Cleland	} 77
1930	J. C. Rose	77
1931	Dr A. Cleland	77
1932	D. M. Stocks .	77
1933	J. S. Graham .	74
1934	{ L. B. Fairbairn { J. C. Rose	} 75
1935	R. Boyack	76
1936	Dr A. Cleland	75
1937	D. S. Weir	75
1938	L. B. Fairbairn	76
1939	R. Boyack	76
1940-45	Second World War Period	..
1946	T. McIlwrick	78

1947	J. S. Johnston. T. McIlwrick .	80
1948	G. L. Stewart.	75
1949	C. Drummond Stevenson	73
1950	A. J. D. Blaikie	74
1951	R. Boyack Dr A. Cleland. T. S. Henderson	77
1952	A. W. Small J. A. Lang R. Wight .	71
1953	A. K. Fleming	73
1954	M. H. Cullen . D. S. Dougal . J. Milne J. S. Robertson	73
1955	Dr D. R. Sandison.	73
1956	A. J. D. Blaikie	73
1957	Dr D. R. Sandison. T. C. Scott W. A. Whitelaw	74
1958	D. S. Lowe	76
1959	D. S. Lowe	73
1960	Dr A. G. Donald	75
1961	J. A. Lang	73
1962	J. R. Ness	74
1963	R. W. Gardiner	75
1964	H. V. Stone	74
1965	J. A. Armstrong	72
1966	A. J. D. Blaikie	74
1967	W. O. Maguire T. Gray .	72
1968	T. Gray . J. Leckie . W. O. Maguire	74
1969	C. T. Rankin .	73
1970	W. G. Carnie . A. W. Small . H. V. Stone .	75
1971	R. R. Jack	77
1972	T. Gray . W. G. Carnie .	75
1973	J. R. Inglis	72
1974	J. R. Inglis	75
1975	J. A. Armstrong	74
1976	W. W. Auld .	76

1977	I. D. Mackenzie	75
1978	R. T. Hamilton M. J. P. Healy	73
1979	J. R. Inglis . M. S. J. McEwan .	78
1980	R. T. Hamilton I. M. Paterson	75
1981	W. D. Henderson	77
1982	R. E. Simpson	75
1983	A. F. Dawson. J. R. Inglis . L. D. Mitchell.	76
1984	L. D. Mitchell J. R. Inglis	74
1985	F. Davidson	77
1986	H. Graham . C. Cuthbert .	75
1987	A. R. Corbett	75
1988	M. B. Livingston	74
1989	J. R. Inglis	68
1990	T. M. Lamb . J. M. Croall . C. E. Paterson	74
1991	J. H. Dobson	71
1992	D. P. Allan	76
1993	J. D. D. Elvin	78

THE COOPER CUP PRESENTED IN 1949 BY
J. M. COOPER FOR THE BEST HANDICAP SCORE AT THE
SUMMER MEETING

		Strokes *Net*
1949	J. A. Scott	70
1950	Dr M. C. K. Finlayson	69
1951	J. H. Annan	64
1952	C. H. Johnston	69
1953	C. D. Watson	65
1954	D. S. Anderson	66
1955	M. T. Scobie	65
1956	I. Macdonald	63
1957	R. P. S. Jones	62
1958	C. G. Wallace, Jr.	63
1959	Dr M. C. K. Finlayson	63
1960	E. G. M. More	64
1961	J. S. Jeffrey	62
1962	D. R. J. Stewart	64
1963	J. Ross	66
1964	D. L. Millar	64
1965	D. G. Kennedy	65
1966	K. W. Paterson-Brown	65
1967	A. R. Anderson	65
1968	W. D. Henderson	61
1969	M. R. Dewar	65
1970	A. J. Dobbie	65
1971	{ K. S. Holmes / W. J. Kinloch Anderson }	64
1972	J. C. Walker	62
1973	K. M. Duncan	64
1974	J. D. Menzies	65
1975	{ M. R. Dewar / A. D. Macintyre }	63
1976	M. J. Bell	61
1977	{ W. D. Henderson / R. G. Kelly }	64
1978	{ W. Grieve / L. W. McConachie / Dr G. Kennedy }	63
1979	{ Lt.-Col. W. H. Chapman / R. K. Martin }	67
1980	A. S. Gray	62
1981	J. A. M. Snow	64
1982	W. A. W. Miller	64

1983	{ R. Mejka .	} 62
	{ I. M. Paterson	
1984	P. C. Shanks .	60
1985	A. D. Macintyre	66
1986	M. Millar.	65
1987	J. J. Degnan .	65
1988	G. R. T. Baird	61
1989	A. C. Dempster	61
1990	A. C. Dempster	63
1991	J. R. Inglis	64
1992	H. R. Nobbs .	61
1993	D. C. Scott	64

THE WELLS BOWL PRESENTED IN 1952 BY
JOHN S. WELLS TO THE WINNERS OF THE
WINTER FOURSOMES

1952-53	J. G. Kynoch and J. H. Campbell, Jr.
1953-54	Dr A. Cleland and Dr F. C. Laing
1954-55	J. Graham and A. W. Small
1955-56	A. K. Fleming and J. Leckie
1956-57	H. J. Porteous and R. Wight
1957-58	A. K. Fleming and J. Leckie
1958-59	I. S. Dougal and J. Ross
1959-60	Dr A. G. Donald and E. G. M. More
1960-61	G. L. Walls and W. A. Whitelaw
1961-62	G. L. Walls and W. A. Whitelaw
1962-63	F. D. Burnet and J. M. Peat
1963-64	I. S. Dougal and J. Ross
1964-65	A. C. Rankin and D. R. J. Stewart
1965-66	Dr M. F. Grieve and G. G. Thomson
1966-67	A. J. D. Blaikie and T. Gray
1967-68	A. M. Drummond and G. Waters
1968-69	A. J. D. Blaikie and T. Gray
1969-70	H. V. Stone and G. T. Whurr
1970-71	K. W. Paterson-Brown and J. H. Marshall
1971-72	A. F. Dawson and C. R. Sanderson
1972-73	F. D. Burnet and J. M. Peat
1973-74	Dr G. Kennedy and Dr W. A. Cranston
1974-75	Dr A. F. Lang and J. D. Stormonth
1975-76	A. D. W. Hamilton and T. McClung
1976-77	W. A. Cranston and Dr G. Kennedy
1977-78	E. S. Maguire and W. O. Maguire
1978-79	Dr W. A. Cranston and M. J. Muir
1979-80	F. D. Burnet and J. M. Peat
1980-81	D. L. Kerr and V. Lall
1981-82	M. J. P. Healy and R. G. Roxburgh
1982-83	Dr W. D. MacLennan and D. L. Millar
1983-84	Dr A. G. Leitch and J. D. S. Bennett
1984-85	D. L. Kerr and V. Lall
1985-86	J. Forrest and A. C. C. Meldrum
1986-87	N. B. Richardson and R. E. Simpson
1987-88	Lt.-Col. W. H. Chapman and Dr D. Thomson
1988-89	A. S. Mayer and J. N. McNeil
1989-90	I. Smith and J. H. Dobson
1990-91	J. A. M. Snow and Dr G. Kennedy
1991-92	E. Brown and N. Lothian
1992-93	R. McLaren and J. W. Stephenson

THE 1892 CUP PRESENTED BY THE GRANDSON OF
JAMES SMITH OF LEITH WHO WON IT IN 1892, NOW
AWARDED FOR THE BEST AGGREGATE SCRATCH SCORES
AT TWO OF THREE MEETINGS

Strokes

Year	Name	Strokes
1964	C. T. Rankin. A. W. Small.	144
1965	J. Leckie Dr D. R. Sandison	146
1966	T. Gray.	145
1967	W. B. M. Laird	140
1968	W. B. M. Laird	142
1969	A. J. Low	143
1970	T. Gray.	143
1971	R. Reid Jack.	149
1972	K. W. Paterson-Brown	147
1973	Dr A. G. Donald. J. R. Inglis	145
1974	I. M. Paterson	139
1975	J. R. Inglis W. O. Maguire	149
1976	J. M. Croall.	143
1977	J. R. Inglis	148
1978	I. D. Miller	147
1979	J. R. Inglis	145
1980	J. R. Inglis	137
1981	J. R. Inglis	146
1982	J. R. Inglis	147
1983	J. R. Inglis	143
1984	J. R. Inglis	141
1985	J. R. Inglis	152
1986	C. Cuthbert	153
1987	C. Cuthbert	143
1988	C. Cuthbert	146
1989	J. R. Inglis	138
1990	C. Cuthbert. T. M. Lamb. I. Smith.	145
1991	C. Cuthbert	140
1992	D. P. Allan R. M. Gaunt.	141
1993	I. Smith.	144

THE MARSHALL QUAICH PRESENTED IN 1970 BY
R. I. MARSHALL FOR THE BEST HANDICAP SCORE FOR
MEMBERS OVER 60

		Strokes Net
1970	A. J. Dobbie	65
1971	W. J. K. Anderson	64
1972	J. S. Deane	64
1973	E. W. Brown	67
1974	I. Maclean	67
1975	R. H. Gardiner / G. B. Hendry	65
1976	A. G. Graham	64
1977	J. Y. Ferguson	68
1978	W. Grieve	63
1979	Lt.-Col. W. H. Chapman	67
1980	P. W. N. Fraser	63
1981	R. B. Legget / R. Aitken	66
1982	W. A. W. Miller	64
1983	Dr D. R. Sandison	66
1984	G. W. Foote	61
1985	J. McLean	67
1986	T. C. Brown	67
1987	F. D. Burnet	67
1988	D. M. Dudgeon	66
1989	H. L. McKill	66
1990	H. L. McKill	67
1991	Dr G. Kennedy	65
1992	R. M. Stewart	66
1993	R. M. Stewart	69

THE CHALMERS QUAICH PRESENTED IN 1977 BY Mrs CHALMERS IN MEMORY OF HER HUSBAND Mr W. M. CHALMERS FOR THE WINNERS OF THE INVITATION FOURSOMES

1977	P. N. Paterson-Brown and A. C. Baird	34 pts
1978	C. G. Wallace and G. MacGregor	33 pts
1979	P. F. Bruce and B. Marshall	38 pts
1980	G. J. Trigger and E. Hood	38 pts
1981	G. G. Williamson and J. McL. Ross	37 pts
1982	A. G. Scott and W. McLure	31 pts
1983	W. D. MacLennan and J. McL. Ross	35 pts
1984	A. R. Corbett and C. A. P. Herd	33 pts
1985	G. W. Tait and J. Douglas	38 pts
1986	C. Marshall and W. Brown	36 pts
1987	A. C. C. Meldrum and A. F. Dawson	33 pts
1988	R. L. Hutchison and W. J. Rogers	37 pts
1989	I. Smith and A. F. Hinds	38 pts
1990	C. Cuthbert and G. Cuthbert	38 pts
1991	A. R. Corbett and I. S. Gray	39 pts
1992	G. K. Lawson and P. Brooks	36 pts
1993	D. L. Murray and W. D. Slater	38 pts

THE MAYER GOBLET PRESENTED IN 1979 BY
W. D. AND M. D. MAYER TO THE WINNERS OF THE
FOUNDATION FOURSOMES

1979	A. H. Lamont and I. R. J. Di Rollo . . .	36 pts
1980	A. B Wilson and A. Douglas	36 pts
1981	C. Marshall and R. A. Kilgour	36 pts
1982	W. D. Henderson and D. M. Kidd . . .	40 pts
1983	P. W. N. Fraser and M. C. Leslie . . .	36 pts
1984	I. Macpherson and V. Lall	43 pts
1985	M. C. Leslie and D. M. Fraser	40 pts
1986	Dr G. Kennedy and D. W. Provan . . .	39 pts
1987	J. N. Croall and A. R. Corbett	36 pts
1988	Dr G. Kennedy and D. W. Provan . . .	38 pts
1989	R. Cumming and A. D. McIntyre . . .	38 pts
1990	K. G. Cameron and G. Cooper	37 pts
1991	{ D. G. Cameron and R. Cumming . . . } { J. T. Williamson and H. L. McKill . . . }	38 pts
1992	D. W. Provan and J. Macrae. . . .	38 pts
1993	A. S. Mayer and A. G. Bennett	36 pts

ACKNOWLEDGEMENTS

No book can be written without assistance, and this one, which is indeed a "team effort", would never have been completed otherwise. My editorial colleagues have been of immense help, and I am truly indebted to James Falconer, Bill Rankine and Buster Wallace for all their support.

Every contributor has given generously of time and effort. In the circumstances it would be incongruous if I was to endeavour to single out any individual by name, but many of our Luffness New Members are included. They have all been most anxious to give assistance, and their contributions have been very much appreciated.

To Les Gibb for his acrylic and pastel painting which was used for the book jacket, and which he generously gifted to the Club; and to Peter Melville, who spent many hours preparing the vignettes and the sundry sketches—thank you both most sincerely.

Archie Baird, an author in his own right, has given me much encouragement and support since the inception of this book, and I am grateful to him for his kindness to me.

The Secretary Ian Tedford and his patient and tolerant Assistant Secretary Fiona Verth have co-operated throughout this publication, often in difficult circumstances, and we are delighted to be able to express our sincere thanks to them both for their unstinting efforts on our behalf.

Last, but by no means least, the Printers Macdonald Lindsay Pindar plc, and in particular Ian McNee, who is "one of us", have cajoled me throughout with courtesy and with good humour.

This venture has been a labour of love, made so much easier by the support which has been forthcoming from everyone concerned with it. If, on reflection, you have found even one item of interest in reading this book, that is our reward. Within these pages we have endeavoured to share with you the pride and pleasure which is experienced by every Member of Luffness New Golf Club.

W. Donald MacLennan,
Editor.

Photoset in Palacio
Made and printed in Great Britain by
Macdonald Lindsay Pindar plc
Edgefield Road, Loanhead,
Midlothian EH20 9SY

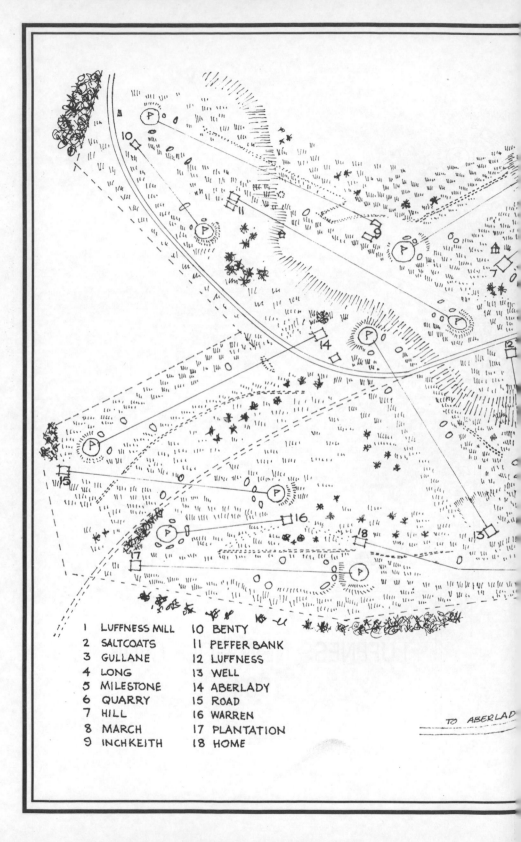

1	LUFFNESS MILL	10 BENTY
2	SALTCOATS	11 PEFFER BANK
3	GULLANE	12 LUFFNESS
4	LONG	13 WELL
5	MILESTONE	14 ABERLADY
6	QUARRY	15 ROAD
7	HILL	16 WARREN
8	MARCH	17 PLANTATION
9	INCHKEITH	18 HOME

TO ABERLAD